Mohamed's Dream:

Overcoming tragedy & cover up from the Midwest to West Africa

by Jon Kerr

Old Man River Press

Preface

"Life is not a matter of holding good cards, but sometimes playing a poor hand well."

Rarely has a fortune cookie proverb been more fitting than this that I opened at a Chinese restaurant during my first interview with Lancine and Madosu Fofana for this book. As parents who had lost their eldest child in unbelievably tragic fashion, they might well have been crushed , embittered and reluctant to talk with a writer. Their experiences with media and government officials could have left them wary of ever again sharing information about their son, their emotions and personal lives.

But the Fofanas never backed away from any subjects regarding an obviously painful experience. They responded with patience to even the most uninformed questions about their immigrant backgrounds and Islamic beliefs. Nearly five years after Mohamed's death in Lilydale Park, we visited the area together. It was his parents first return in that time. We also went together to Mohamed's grave site. Their generosity, as well as their quiet bravery and strength of character and faith was stunning. I am immensely appreciative and honored to have gotten to know them.

I have my own sense of loss attached to this story, though of course nothing near to that suffered by the Fofanas. As one of the leaders of a volunteer community group focused on Lilydale Park, we saw an area we loved become a place of tragedy and vilification. That the vilification was often based on false premises added insult to injury. Our trust in, and relationship with, some Saint Paul city leaders was broken beyond repair and the organization's civic efforts ground to a halt.

I did not become involved with this story as a professional journalist, although I believe the skills I have developed in that capacity have greatly aided me in researching and telling this story, along with inside information gained about Lilydale Park through my years of involvement with the Friends of Lilydale Park

I also believe this subject is an example of the limitations that often afflict journalism in this era with significant staff cutbacks, the 24-hour news cycle and haste to move onto new subject matter. The current state of journalism unfortunately tends to lead to reliance on easily-sought-out official sources and explanations. Activists, with their demands for investigation and spending scarce time on digging deeper, easily become seen as an annoyance. The result is too often a reversal of the famous saying that the role of media is to comfort the afflicted and afflict the comfortable.

As the tragedy that began with the two boys deaths continued, I was left with a taste in my mouth that can sometimes still be difficult to swallow. I'm not sure I can ever be as quietly forgiving as the Fofanas, though I also believe that setting the historical record straight is a public need that then can allow for closure and positive efforts to ensure such events are never repeated.

But the Fofanas' examples taught me. Their ability to rise above pain and demonstrate how to positively go forward in life has been inspirational.

I was able to travel to Guinea, West Africa with Mohamed's father, Lancine, and had opportunity to meet other family members. We saw the place where they are building a school and community center in Mohamed's honor. I am again deeply grateful for the lessons they have taught me and the chance they and others have created for this story to have a silver lining of hope and focus on the benefit to others.

Gratitude and appreciation must also go to others who have joined efforts to go beyond race and cultural differences. This includes many who have backed me in this writing and publication effort. Special thanks to Grit Youngquist, Sarah Snapp, David Stanford, Don Jacobson, Rachel Anderson, Kurt Swanson, David Sullivan-Nightengale, Forrest Smith, Barbara Larcom, *City Pages,* Laurie Stern, Interfaith Service to Latin America, and others. Financial and moral support from Jane Rinehart, Joelle Tegwen, Corinne Smith, Timothy Church, Jeffrey Erdmann, Thomas Goldstein, Cheick M cherif Keita, Aboubacar Camara, Lois Quam, Kathleen Brotham, Preetmohinder Sidhu, and Marty Hicks.

Nothing can change what happened in Lilydale Park on May 22, 2013. But hopefully this account will help increase understanding and also help prevent similar events in the future. This would also be an outcome that would honor Mohamed.

Mohamed's Dream

Timeline

1983 – Saint Paul takes over full control of Lilydale Park after Brickyard & bluff mining closed, residents removed.

1999 – Friends of Lilydale Park is formed, will warn of bluff instability at Ventoss View, 911 issues in park.

2003 – Immigrants Madosu & Lancine marry, son Mohamed is born. Will attend Peter Hobart Elementary.

2009 – City consultant warns of Lilydale Park bluff instability, urges further study at cost of $10-$12,000.

2011 – Major landslide on North Knob bluff in Lilydale.

2012 – St. Paul Parks & Public Works staff start work on Cherokee storm-water culvert despite erosion warnings.

May 22, 2013 – Landslide kills 2, injures 2, & scars entire group of fossil hunting students in Lilydale Park.

Sept. 12, 2013 – NTI & Donald Lewis' "independent investigation" calls landslide unpredictable. Same day city emails describe major storm-water erosion issues.

Oct. 2013 – DNR hydrologist Dr. Carrie Jennings points to Cherokee culvert storm-water as likely landslide cause.

Jan. 2014 – City quietly starts multi-million $$ plans to reengineer Cherokee culvert & accident site area.

Feb. 2014 – City agrees to $1M closed landslide legal settlement. Mohamed's parents give funds toward his dream of African school & programs.

Introduction

I overcame the nightmares because of my dreams.

– Jonas Salk

T his is a story of a nightmare that became a dream. It is also a story of dishonesty that led to finding of some truths. It is a story of self-interest that led to unselfish concern for others. It is a story of cover-up that led to opening of connections between far distant communities. It is also a story of how a young boy's short life galvanized others and brought some understanding to a world in desperate need of it. This is a story of Mohamed's dream.

Mohamed Fofana was only ten years old on May 22, 2013. While having relatively little life experience, he nevertheless had a wisdom and awareness well beyond his years. This was according to all who knew him. His tragic death, and that of another young person, on that day in 2013 brought understandable sorrow as well as shock to his parents, teachers and school classmates. On that fateful day, not only family and friends, but thousands, perhaps millions, of people around the world heard of it.

But fame can be brief, as Andy Warhol noted. The news cycle soon moved on, with Mohamed joining vast numbers of innocent victims of circumstance in our world who are regularly forgotten - except by those closest to them. Their life aspirations quickly become moot beside the concerns of the more powerful and self-interested who generally write history.

Certainly there were those who were anxious to move on from inconvenient truths about what happened in Lilydale Park. Condolences and platitudes about the unforeseeable injustices of life came from high places while serious inquiries into the event were deliberately limited in scope. Most public servants certainly want to live up to their responsibilities. But evidence that the Peter Hobart Elementary fossil-hunting group might have walked into a death-trap - which Saint Paul officials knew about but failed to act upon - was also buried as they hoped the landslide would fade from memories.

The general public certainly felt strong emotion as they watched images of Mohamed, the other deceased child and their mourning families. The heroic efforts of hundreds of firefighters, police and rescue workers was displayed on radio, newspapers and television by news station helicopters that circled hour upon hour over the Lilydale Park bluffside. That they failed to save Mohamed and the other boy only added to the tragedy of the situation. Universal human compassion was on full display during and after the event, with memorials attracting widespread public attention on at least two continents.

But for most not directly affected, interest understandably faded along with the wilting flowers left by a Lilydale Park entrance near the landslide site. Even those in the neighborhoods surrounding the Saint Paul park seemed ready to move on within a few days. People naturally want to look away from pain and sadness.

They accepted official promises, oft-repeated in compliant local media, that all dangers from unchecked storm-water running over unstable Mississippi River bluffs would soon be addressed. That the problems still remain six years later - even if the city has erected ornate fences that theoretically block off the entire area - is but one more remaining shame.

Curiously, public outrage was more often directed at school officials for allowing the fossil-hunting field trip to a "dangerous" place than to the Saint Paul Parks & Recreation Department even though Parks Department staff were in the best position to know the dangers and perhaps had a better PR strategy. The oft-suggested notion that nature can be cruel was yet another factor. The truly dark side of this story – and its decidedly unnatural origins - has become clear to those who care to see.

As urban parks go, Lilydale Park long seemed an untamed and dangerous place. City planners had begun to bring paved roads, trails, buildings and utilities into an area that community members and activists had loved for its rustic character. The park provided an opportunity to preserve a uniquely natural area and activities in the center of a metropolitan area. That human engineering likely played a major role in the May 22, 2013 event is a tragic irony and a lesson in our cultural unwillingness to remember the past.

Forgotten was the Lilydale area's unique history as a crossroads of natural and human-made influences. The area, carved out tens of thousands of years ago by what was once runoff from glacial Lake Agassiz, included a waterfall three times the size of Niagara Falls in what would become the Mississippi River floodplain. During the quirky Cambrian period, 540 to 490 million years ago, temperatures warmed enough to allow semi-tropical marine life to thrive. Fossilized skeletons from that era would later become a major public attraction, bringing many children and adults to the sandstone river-bluffs of Lilydale Park.

Before this, the area was a hunting ground for Native Americans who utilized the Mississippi as their superhighway. White settlers brought commercial elements, beginning with log-floating. In the late Nineteenth Century the bluffs were mined for material to be fired in kilns and made into bricks. Machines and workers carved unnatural gashes into the hillsides while their children and families enjoyed a rugged, libertarian life in the midst of the remaining natural beauty. Just across the river from downtown Saint Paul and less than two miles from the Minnesota state capitol, the small semi-rural community of Lilydale rose up part Huck Finn and part industrial company town.

Mother Nature would eventually seem to win out when Mississippi River floods forced all remaining residents from the area by the early 1970s. But human impact would not disappear even with the brickyards closed and the area becoming Lilydale Park.

Ironically, Mohamed's family roots were in a not-dissimilar mining area. His father, Lancine, had grown up in the gold-mining fields of Guinea, West Africa. Many young people, as well as the environment, are regularly sacrificed in the hope of quick fortune, but Lancine's father urged him to seek education and opportunity for a better life in the United States. Mohamed's mother, Madosu, survived civil war in her native Liberia and a youth spent in refugee camps before family sponsors made it possible for her to seek the American dream.

Fate brought Lancine and Madosu together in Minnesota with its white-out snowstorms and its sometimes passive-aggressive "nice" responses to a black Islamic family. But their faith, both religious and in the American dream, would carry them through and help them raise children with similar determination to find light even in the darkest periods. The tragic events in Lilydale Park would not dim the beliefs that they had passed on to their children.

That light would shine on a handmade journal that prescient eight-year-old Mohamed made following a trip to the homeland of his parents. Found after his death, it touchingly called for remembering and sharing with those in need. It laid out his personal dreams of spending his life selflessly helping others. He obviously was never personally able to achieve the goals he had written and drawn about in his journal.

Yet Mohamed's spirit lives on. It is manifest in those who had the chance to know him, including parents and family who had already experienced great hardship in their lives, but who refused to descend into bitterness or despair. It is apparent in equally amazing teachers and classmates at Peter Hobart Elementary. And it has spread to other community members and friends who joined the cause to keep Mohamed's dream alive.

Today it is taking physical shape in Guinea at a site where a school is under construction along with a newly-opened community health center. Mohamed's spirit has built a cross-cultural community committed to fulfilling the goals expressed in his journal. It is an ongoing project and process that may or may not realize the lofty goals of its proponents. Life is not all sweetness and light with Hollywood endings.

But the very vision and attempt is both a tribute to Mohamed, an unbelievably generous boy, and an example to the world of how dreams can still come true when people are willing to come together behind them. That was Mohamed's dream.

From birth, Mohamed Fofana was known as a happy, inquisitive child. When his younger, twin brothers Hassan and Al-Semy were born (bottom left) he also became a loving role model

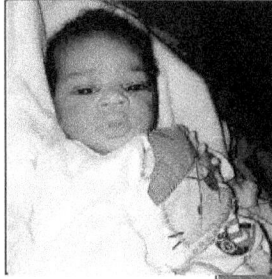

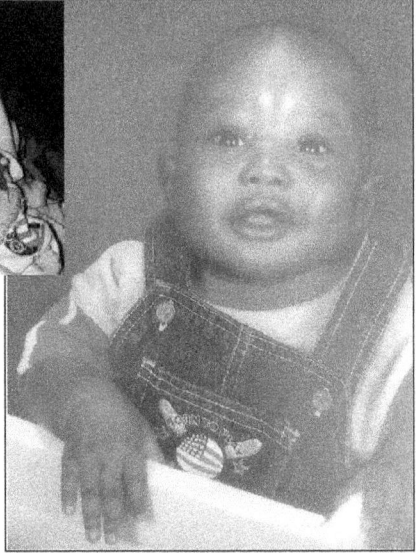

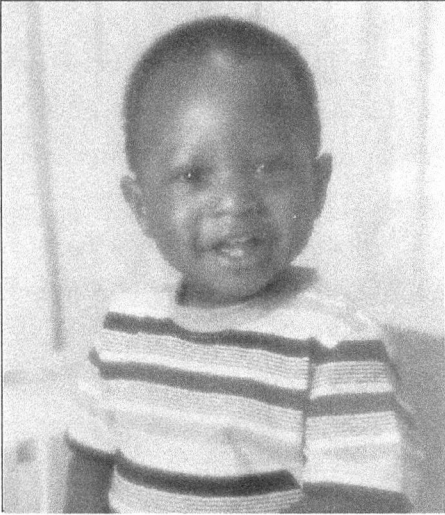

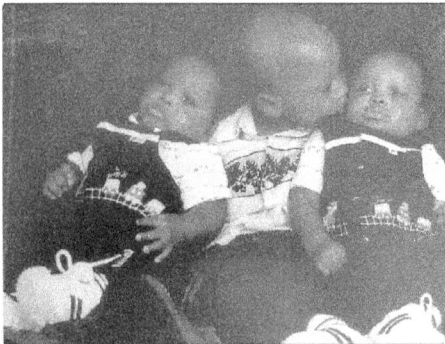

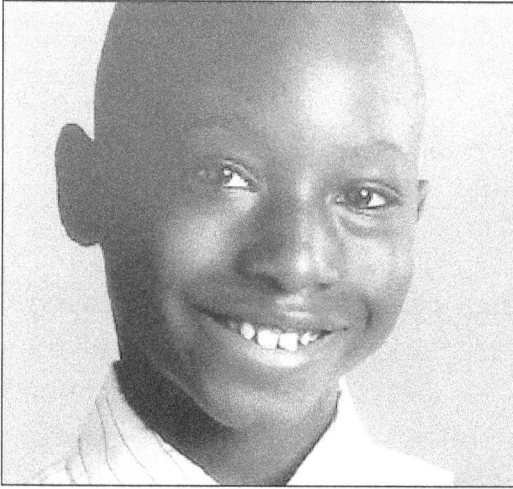

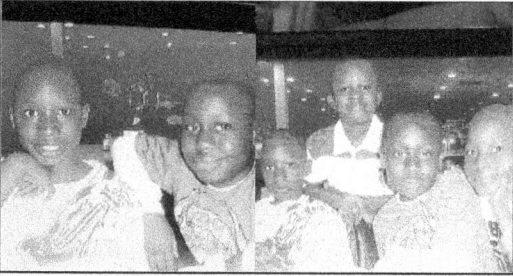

Mohamed was known by family and friends as a happy, fun-loving boy, who from an early age, equally loved sports and academics.

Chapter 1:

"The only thing dark about Africa is our ignorance of it."
George H.T. Kimble, 19th Century geographer

L eaving the airport at Bamako, it is immediately clear that I have entered a different part of the world. Yet, the remnants of French colonization make for a confused mix of what is indigenous to Mali alongside baguettes in restaurants and highway billboards showing ridiculously light-skinned, middle-class families opening bank accounts or buying SUVs.

The French influence in language and culture stands in contrast to the realities of the West African landscape with locals riding two-and-three abreast on moto-scooters while dodging goats and push-cart operators trying to eke out a daily living. Poverty that would make any Paris ghetto appear opulent is everywhere. The material world's harsh demands compete against calls from minarets to remember the centrality of the Muslim spiritual world.

Our anticipated three-hour drive to Siguiri, Guinea, begins in a weathered Toyota sedan crammed with five men and baggage. We drive out of the sprawling Mali capital into arid grasslands under a hazy, rust-colored sunset.

It's a typical dry season day that begins and would end with a clear blue sky except for a blanket of descending Sahara dust. The Harmattan trade winds blowing in from nearly a thousand miles to the north can be seen from space and sometimes force rerouting of aircraft. They are an increasing feature of life in all of western Africa, and now sometimes sweep north to Europe. Occasionally they cross the Atlantic to the Caribbean, Florida, Texas and even as far as California. Amazon basin areas regularly receive iron nutrients from the dust storms which are also believed to stimulate algae growth in the ocean.

While adding color and perhaps a few positive environmental benefits, the Sahara dust usually brings a host of negative health effects to West Africa – particularly when combined with other pollutants that create smog. The most obvious are for those with asthma or other respiratory ailments. Silicosis can result from continued collection of sand particles in lungs. Some studies have noted that the Harmattan winds can also carry chemicals and living microbes that may be dangerous to humans and animals.

There have been few conclusive scientific studies of the winds' impacts to date, perhaps another statement of the relative importance – or lack thereof – of African health to the world economy. However, West Africans certainly have plenty of anecdotal evidence from family, friends and neighbors with various breathing issues and ailments. Even a short-term visitor could feel a slight burning in his throat after a few days.

Nevertheless life goes on with a shrug and smile for most. Locals remain focused on making the best of the hand they have been dealt in an oft-forgotten part of the planet.

As night falls, we drive by a small, historic village that my host, guide and occasional savior, Lancine Fofana, nevertheless proudly points out in the dark. It was the ancestral birthplace of the founder of a Mali Empire that once spanned from Timbuktu to Nigeria and was noted for its trade, culture and educational development. Only after almost 500 years did it break down in the early 17th Century, when European colonial powers swept in to exploit tribal divisions as well as West Africa's resources.

Included were the regions humans, who became the initial source of slave trade to the Americas. It is estimated that up to a third of Mandinka or Mandingo language speakers were enslaved and that the majority of African-Americans have genetic ties to West Africa. The miracle of modern transportation now has made it relatively easy for some, along with more recent, voluntary immigrants to return, as Lancine was now doing. He allowed me to tag along.

Our drive through largely rural, scrub-brush terrain - with windows rolled down to help fend off nearly 90-degree heat even at sunset - was largely uneventful. Stereotypical Western fears of highway bandits, or terrorist attacks and kidnappings began to fade from my mind in the midst of the good-natured welcome from my Fofana family hosts. The surprisingly well-conditioned road began to feel as tame as any Minnesota stretch of highway in the summertime. I relaxed into the rhythm of the car wheels and the occasionally dotted yellow-line in front of me.

Suddenly, out of the dark, a large-horned cow – or bull - appeared on my side of the vehicle as we approached a curve. The feeling of danger was not unfamiliar to anyone driving at dusk in many rural areas of the Midwest United States.

But unlike a deer, the animal did not freeze in the headlights. Instead, the bovine lowered his head and horns while rapidly coming on strong at an angle that looked certain to intersect with either the front windshield or my passenger-side window. For a moment I envisioned myself as unwitting matador - without any sword for defense.

Fortunately our driver, Lancine's half-brother Mamadi, was wide awake and alert. He was able to skillfully swerve to the gravel on the other side of the road, saving all involved from serious physical injury. Only the side-view mirror was a casualty on this occasion, flying into my hands and briefly making me wonder in the dark if I had been handed part of the cow/bull's anatomy.

But all mammals survived this classically Third World encounter with fate. We drove on with Mamadi laughing uproariously and my face now probably looking even whiter in the near-total darkness of the night.

Mamadi and Lancine's light-hearted natures were put to a more severe test as we crossed the Mali-Guinea border making stops at dimly-lit offices. Officials sweating in the heat, examining our papers with heightened interest and some surprise at seeing a United States passport. It went slowly, but generally without incident. One agent pointed out their need for a working fan, let alone a computer, a somewhat obvious hint which was easily accommodated with a small gift. All part of the cost of doing business, so to speak.

Redundant stops seemed designed to employ a few more border officials. It was relatively painless, if needlessly time consuming and inefficient by standards of the Western world. We moved on and were approaching the final wooden barricade when suddenly a Guinean officer became notably upset, waving a gun and shouting at us to stop. We had apparently driven past a nonexistent stop sign at his picnic table post.

A heated exchange followed which left this non-French speaker watching helplessly as more uniformed, and armed officers joined the kerfuffle. Lancine and then Mamadi became alternately animated and conciliatory, with unclear effect, in an argument that went on for at least 15 minutes.

Suddenly everyone broke into smiles and friendly greetings. The previously agitated officer turned and in English welcomed me to Guinea. I smiled and nodded in dumbfounded confusion. As we drove away, Lancine filled me in on what had transpired and what I would also learn to be a central connecting thread of West African culture.

"He realized we were family," explained Lancine of the border officer's sudden change of attitude. "His mother was a Fofana. We are all Fofanas."

****

Family is everything, they say, and nowhere is that likely more true than in Guinea.

Clan or family lineage can be recited back for multiple generations, even if seldom formally recorded on paper. Storytellers, or oral historians called griots, have been a central part of cultural traditions since they literally sang the praises of Mali rulers. Their knowledge and role of court historians also made them valued counselors.

The Mali empire has long since disappeared, but not the respect for griots. They no longer have official roles, yet remain valued figures in nearly every Guinean village. For the right price, even a commoner like myself can now get their own West African version of a LinkedIn biography presented with great fanfare at a public gathering.

Mostly however, family connection was more subtly remembered in daily life. For Lancine it was clearly one of the most important and unbroken links to a world he physically left behind decades ago. Almost as soon as we arrived in Siguiri, his cellphone began ringing. Everywhere we went, multiple brothers, sisters, aunts and uncles would show up with affectionate greetings.

It seemed impossible that the family tree could be rooted so tightly. But in Guinea, I soon learned, there was no such thing as a cousin – which is considered too distant a term. Every relative is seemingly an intimate one.

"How could I not miss this? I wait two years for this visit," Lancine said, smiling broadly. Not that his wife and two sons back in Minnesota - with whom he talked by telephone almost daily – weren't greatly missed while traveling to Africa. "It is always coming home even though it is many years since I lived here."

Lancine's prodigal son, or sette' status, was hardly unique in Guinea, or indeed many other parts of the developing world. Remittances – money sent back – is a huge part of the global economy.

But Lancine's remembrance of his homeland and willingness to travel long miles to visit was clearly appreciated in its own right. Family bonds clearly stretched over distance and time. It even included a foreign visitor, who was immediately accepted into the Fofana family because of connection to Lancine. My honor was unofficial but repeatedly mentioned in warm welcomes.

Family bonds clearly extended to Lancine's second, or non-birth, mother - his father's second wife, whom he visited almost immediately after seeing his birth mother. The common West African practice of men having multiple wives dates to before Islam came to the region, with more children seen as a necessary measure to ensure continuation of the family lineage. The prophet Muhammad put limits on the number of wives any man could have, with strict responsibility for providing for them and all children a further obligation on the man.

It clearly wasn't an issue in the Fofana family. While hardly wealthy, Lancine's family is probably part of Guinea's small middle class. Most in Siguiri have to be entrepreneurial to survive, with the result being streets lined with stalls and peddlers selling anything from vegetables to used clothing to handmade wooden items to bottles of gasoline for motorcycles. It is generally a life of hard labor, long, hot hours and widespread poverty. But the Fofanas appeared to have done relatively well, owning modest hotels, restaurants and other small businesses.

Lancine's father, Sekou, I learned, eked out some success as first a small rice farmer in the arid, red soil. Then he moved into renting out equipment needed by the region's increasing number of small "artisan" gold miners. The boom started 40 some years ago as Siguiri began to attract those dreaming of fortune - or at least some hope of making enough to survive.

With the coming of multi-national mining operations in the last decade, the town of roughly 30,000 has grown to a population of nearly 200,000. Most live in ramshackle housing that sprawls out into the bush areas. Some live right in the gold-mining area without access to running water, electricity or any public services.

Logic might have called for Sekou's four sons to follow him into the family business, splitting up the land and profits. But he foresaw a different future for them, recognizing that climatic and social change were creating ever more unstable conditions in Guinea. Rainfall patterns in particular were becoming irregular, as witnessed by the yearly dry season dust bowl that was formerly the Niger River. The situation is worsened by floods that wash through the whole area during the rainy season.

"The goal of my dad was to send all the kids to school," recalled Lancine, also referring to his four sisters. "We always asked him why not stay on the farm? But he wanted different options for us. He saw that farming was unstable, and the mining business too. Water comes and it goes. The gold too."

The desire for quick riches exists in Guinea. as in all cultures. But the Fofana family chose instead to think longer-term. Mohamed's grandfather decided to invest in an alternate future that some in his situation might have considered foolish. Schools remain far from a sure-fire bet in most developing countries.

Yet the value of education was clearly a priority and value that Lancine learned early on. Going to school was not possible for many, but his father always made sure he and his brothers and sisters had the supplies, uniforms and other essentials they needed to attend a semi-public institution. There they studied hard sciences and mathematics as well as French and Islam.

"We were lucky to have a father who could and would support us in learning and school. We weren't rich. But we had shoes and clothing unlike some others," Lancine remembered, in contrast to the children his age that he would see working in the gold-mining fields. He would come to recognize how lucky he was. Education as a path out of poverty was not a dream that many Guineans of his generation could envision.

A visitor to Siguiri would find the situation had changed little, and had likely worsened, some forty years later.

Children as young as six or seven could be seen working long hours in the sun hauling buckets of dirt, carrying heavy metal detectors or doing other chores. Women's responsibilities include sifting pans of dirt in water hoping to find a few nuggets of gold that might pay for food. The men, particularly younger ones, were the underground miners hand digging shafts down, then outward in narrow, dark, one-person tunnels following gold veins wherever they would lead. Exhausting manual labor each and every day leaves little time or energy for school and other activities.

Entire families could be seen engaged in literally overturning huge, barren areas of land that looked like moonscapes or scenes from World War I. They would stand over or climb into small holes in the ground, hoping to find a small miracle hidden somewhere in the underworld.

Almost as often they find tragedy in some form. Cave-ins are a regular event in the unregulated enterprise of artisan gold mining, as over-eager diggers often undermine each other's shafts with sometimes disastrous results. There are no rescue crews, equipment or ambulances available. Just a few years earlier 16 miners were killed near Siguiri in one accident alone.

The dangers don't end when back above ground and can extend to the wider community. Extraction of gold from rocks is often done with toxic chemicals including mercury that can cause serious neurological and brain damage not only to miners but to anyone within miles. Mercury rapidly vaporizes in the African heat and can be carried great distances by air currents. Additional risks include TB, lung cancer and other severe respiratory ailments from all the dust. Safer mining methods are possible but unaffordable for most artisanal miners.

Violence is another part of the desperate life in gold rush areas. An armed battle between two competing groups at the Guinea-Mali border resulted in 17 deaths just before Christmas 2017. Prostitution, human trafficking and other exploitation is also common.

Similar events happen in many parts of the developing world. The number of victims amongst the estimated 30 million artisanal miners - including up to 600,000 poor children worldwide - is unknown. Again, there appears to be little interest in the developed world to learn of such incidental costs for gold. But it is clear that few, if any, of the children who are miners in Siguiri will ever be able to attend school or have any opportunity for a different life.

"Sometimes I think about those kids and I can't sleep," said Lancine, shaking his head sadly. "They start at maybe (age) seven and go to 70, if they live, and never go to school, never have a chance."

The Wild West atmosphere in gold rush areas like Siguiri has been only partly controlled by the coming of international mining operations which are given huge "concession" areas of land by government officials. These often come with the forceful removal of independent artisan miners and sometimes entire local villages. In 2015 and 2016 approximately 380 households not far from Siguiri were forcibly evicted from their ancestral lands by soldiers backed by a World Bank and U.S. pension-fund supported project. Only after some international pressure did many receive any kind of compensation.

On the positive side, it is true that the resulting huge open-pit mines certainly provide many needed jobs at what are relatively good wages. But most workers don't realize, or must overlook, serious health risks from heavy machinery operations, particularly in the processing of the gold ore. This time, rather than mercury, it is the use of cyanide in massive filtration ponds that can result in long-term dangers – especially when the chemical escapes into local aquifers or other water supplies. It can only be hoped that when international mining company AngloGold is finished with digging out the area near Siguiri that it will live up to promises of environmental cleanup.

We met with activists and advocates for miners. Their lack of resources combined with Guinea's weak oversight laws and corruption mean their only hope may be to turn international pressure on the gold industry. Siguiri's resources, also including major bauxite (aluminum) mines located not far away, ultimately belong not to them. Africa's still semi-colonial status helps pay for the good life for others in the world, even if most of us are generally unaware how are blessings are achieved.

"We have so many problems here, and throughout Africa. I don't know how it will change," concluded Lancine with uncharacteristic pessimism.

It is difficult to know how many Guineans are aware of their exploitation though they have gone through periods, especially after independence from France in 1958, of strident political activism. The nation's founder, Sekou Toure, was a leader in Pan-African socialism and sought to find a middle ground between the competing East and West during the Cold War. An immediate reaction was the French pulling out all financial, educational and social infrastructure, leaving Guinea one of the most impoverished nations on earth. They still have not recovered even though they are now considered a U.S. ally.

There is amazingly little, at least visible, animosity toward a white-skinned visitor. Instead there seems to perhaps be almost a shrugging, complacent attitude from many Siguiri residents that is perhaps a pragmatic response to history. They have learned to smile in the face of hardship and adopt a sometimes fatalistic Islamic philosophy of accepting God's will as a logical response to factors of climate, politics and life beyond their control.

Lancine clearly knows his country's history and his own good fortune. The dangers of mining and the risk of being buried under tons of dirt was a part of everyday life that the Fofanas of his generation seemingly avoided. That his son, Mohamed, would suffer that fate in a place so many miles and timezones from Siguiri was to be a bitter irony. But expectations for the entire family had been changed - with gratitude, rather than regret, becoming an emotional base.

"My father tried everything to make sure we could go to school and avoid being in the mines," said Lancine, who after graduating high school went on to study at a vocational school in Conakry, the capital of Guinea. "It wasn't just for us, it was for the future of the whole family."

Mohamed's grandfather, whom he never met, clearly took seriously the investment he had made.

"He'd even check up on us at school. But thank God we never got in trouble. As a result we were able to have choices in life," Lancine said proudly. "It was what eventually brought me to America and the life I always wanted for my own children."

*****

Lancine's story of perseverance is matched, if not exceeded, by that of his wife, Madosu, Mohamed's mother.

Madosu Kennah was born the second of eight children in her family on a small coffee & cacao farm across the Guinean border to the southeast in Liberia. It was a modest but happy lifestyle. A houseful of children no doubt provided many challenges for her parents, but at least there was plenty of home-grown laborers who quickly learned a work ethic.

"After school every day we'd all go to the farm to pick coffee and cacao," remembered Madosu. "It was hard but we knew we needed to learn how to do things. My dad said I'm not going to live forever so I want you to learn how to be independent."

Not that it was all hard work and no play on their five-acre farm in a small rural community.

"We had fun. It was a quiet and everybody in our town was friendly," she said with a smile, recalling growing up during the 1980s. "We had no problems with anyone."

Then everything changed in 1990 as Liberia's unique historical tensions bubbled over into a brutal civil war. Over 250,000 people would eventually lose their lives in a conflict that pitted ethnic factions against each other. Atrocities against civilians were regularly committed by multiple armed groups, each fighting for power in alliances that could change overnight. To Americans, and probably much of the world, it appeared an almost inscrutable battle of egos and grudges led by figures with names such as Samuel Doe, Prince Johnson and Charles Taylor.

But its roots might well be traced back to Liberia's pre-Civil War origins as an ill-conceived solution to U.S. slavery problems. Believing they could end America's growing divisions, abolitionist leaders and others - including Thomas Jefferson and a young Abraham Lincoln - advocated for a radical social experiment. The naive and racist solution they fell upon called for sending former slaves back to Africa. Left untouched was the actual institution of slavery.

Today it is difficult to understand how this Back to Africa movement could ever have been taken seriously. Yet for a time in early 19th Century the concept gained widespread support. Even some southern plantation owners backed the plan – seeking to rid the nation of free blacks who they feared might encourage slave uprisings.

Of course, this master plan to reverse human trafficking across the Atlantic ran into the immediate problem of where to send thousands of people who by now had little knowledge, language or other contacts with their ancestral homes. Generations had passed and slaves from different parts of Africa had been strongly encouraged – by fear of the lash or even death - to forget their past.

But in 1820 The American Colonization Society (ACS) coerced a local chief to sell them a strip of what was then known as the Grain Coast between Guinea and the British colony of Sierra Leone. It was the start of a land grab that theoretically gave new opportunity for free blacks and former slaves - but which came at a high price.

Few freed slaves had skills, knowledge or other resources that prepared them for the challenges they faced in Africa. The high mortality rates among colonizers due to disease, lack of medicine, food and other harsh conditions didn't deter organizers from sending thousands of black Americans to a place that for them was unfamiliar and increasingly hostile. The racism that was at the root of the original idea was carried forward into the entire undertaking, with predictably painful results.

From the beginning, there were clashes with indigenous peoples who, for obvious reasons resented the newcomers. The unwitting colonists became known as Americo-Liberians and were often of mixed-race including European blood. Culturally they were distinct in their education, religion and culture – making English the official language - and they did not identify with the indigenous, non-Christian peoples.

When the ACS went bankrupt in 1847, Liberia's colonists were directed to declare themselves a free and independent state, adopting a constitution patterned after that of the U.S. Though a small minority, their control of the government in the capital of Monrovia would last for the next 133 years based on a racist view of the world that reflected the life they had known as slaves. The Americo-Liberians essentially created a caste system with themselves at the top and indigenous Liberians at the bottom. Voting and other rights only came to all residents of Liberia as they became "civilized" through western-style education and conversion to Christianity.

The suppression of indigenous Liberians required U.S. intervention on several occasions. This was arguably more to protect corporate interests than any loyalty to former slaves or freed blacks. Geopolitical interests kept U.S. military bases in the country through World War II.

It wasn't a situation that could end well. In 1980 a little known Liberian Army sergeant named Samuel Doe led a bloody coup that threw the entire power structure into disarray. His government's abuses of power and corruption on behalf of his minority tribe led to counter-revolution in 1985 by other ethnic groups and civil war that lasted almost 20 years. It was an incredibly brutal period with atrocities committed on all sides.

Madosu's family was among the thousands of innocent people who were forced to flee their homes at risk of death. One night they learned that a band of armed men, with a reputation for ruthless killing and raping of anyone they encountered, were coming to their part of Liberia.

"They weren't picking and choosing," she said, remembering the fear and necessity to quickly pack only what they could carry on their backs. Her family walked two days and nights to make it across the Sierra Leone border, where they thought they would be safe. Little did they realize that the war would soon also spread across that border due to tribal and other connections.

"You had to run for your life," recalled Madosu, who was only age 11 at the time. "Then we came to Sierra Leone and we had to run again."

It was an experience that could permanently scar anyone. But Madosu has managed to balance it with memories of the kindnesses that so many average people in small towns and farming communities showed them and many other refugees.

"We didn't know anybody there. {Yet) all the people took us in and gave us food, water, a place to sleep – no charge," she remembered with gratitude. "It didn't matter if we were Christian or Muslim. We all were welcomed and did everything together."

After months of itinerant life and living off the kindness of strangers, Madosu's family finally made it to a newly-established United Nations refugee camp in Guinea. Little did they know it would become their home for nearly nine years as civil war continued to rage in Liberia and almost the entire West Africa region.

"It was a huge place," said Madosu of the camp, which supplied only the most basic housing, food and medical care. No one knew how long the war might last nor that the number of refugees would run into the hundreds of thousands. "They tried their best to take care of us but it was tough sometimes."

Shipments of supplies officially came every two months. However sometimes the shipments were delayed or didn't come at all. Then the entire camp population had to make do with whatever food they could find for themselves. Madosu remembered planting and raising vegetables on a small plot which grew to eventually supply a large part of the family's diet.

She also recalled regular electricity shortages that required her to use candles and other home-made light sources to do her schoolwork at night. Yet with her parents' encouragement, she persevered and took advantage of the refugee camp school. Madosu would eventually get her high school diploma. She was ready to move on to bigger and better things, and held the same kinds of dreams any graduate might have.

But life in a refugee camp doesn't often allow normal life options. Madosu and her family had to wait for someone else to determine their fate. Rumors naturally swirled amongst so many people with limited control over their lives. Fear was always close at hand as civil war continued to rage in Liberia. Optimism about returning home became increasingly difficult as the years passed. The family began turning their sights towards emigration somewhere, anywhere in the world that would take them.

"We were always hoping for the best. But we never knew what would happen," recalled Madosu, now able to calmly look back at the family's nearly nine year wait in the refugee camp.

Then finally in 2000, the family got a break. One of Madosu's brothers was permitted to leave the camp for school in Saudi Arabia. There he became close with someone from the United States. One thing led to another, and Madosu's brother was allowed to come to the States where he could then become an immigration sponsor for the rest of the family. They were all to become Minnesotans.

Memories of the next year are today a happy blur for Madosu, who describes how the family encountered a world they barely knew existed. Travel, via Portugal to New York City, included the first airplane flight ever for Madosu as well as her first encounter with a major metropolitan area.

"It was very amazing. I was very scared at first. All the people and big buildings, I'd never seen anything like it," she said of the experience.

But her family's overall adjustment came fairly easily, partly given their knowledge of the English language and partly due to the assistance given them by earlier Liberian immigrants to the United States. There was also during that time a very different U.S. governmental attitude and policy toward refugees.

"We got a lot of help and classes telling us about the place we were going to. We even had social workers teaching us about all kinds of things like how to ride a bus and other things. Communication was really good and they told us about everything. It still wasn't always easy, but it helped a lot," Madosu said.

Her initial experience entering the U.S. differed from Lancine's arrival as a 21-year-old, a few years earlier in 1995. He was seeking to continue his education as an electrician after graduating from what might be called a junior college in Conakry. He landed first in Boston, where he was held for two hours in immigration simply because there was no one available who spoke French.

From there things only got stranger. Lancine missed connections on arrival in New York City and without speaking any English had to decipher the JFK airport and transportation connections. Fortunately, another recent French-speaking immigrant from Western Africa recognized his dilemma and helped him figure out the bus route to the apartment of a Guinean friend in the city.

"I was very confused for a while with the language and everything else. It was hard but a lot of people helped me," Lancine recalled. "I had a teacher that almost made me her son. My life in America started right there. I think God was with me."

He was indeed fortunate compared to many of the hundreds of Guinean men who came to the U.S. in the 1990s and sometimes faced a more unfriendly reception. Among those was Amadou Diallo, the victim of a notorious 1999 killing. While in the doorway of his Brooklyn home, he was shot 19 times by undercover police in a case of mistaken identity. The execution attracted international media attention with notables such as Rev. Al Sharpton and Johnny Cochrane pushing unsuccessfully for criminal charges against the officers.

Lancine, by contrast, spent almost two peaceful years in New York City studying English, then managing to get a green card that allowed him to work. But it was still challenging for him to truly get used to big city life. When a Guinean friend who had moved to Minneapolis told him about a job opportunity there, Lancine thought it sounded like a great idea. Taking a Greyhound bus cross-country, he arrived just in time for a November 1996 snowstorm.

"It was really hard to adapt to the cold. I didn't have a heavy coat or boots," remembered Lancine. "A lot of things were different. People were not used to meeting Africans and were confused about Guinea," he added, referring to common confusion of his homeland with the south Pacific island nation of New Guinea.

"But most people were really nice. I've never had any serious problems," he said, quickly pushing past memories of offensive comments by a few fellow workers about his Muslim faith. "But I never want to report anyone and get them fired. I believe we can usually work everything out when people get to know each other."

His own tolerance and upbeat attitude has likely been the key to making that happen more often than not.

Everything certainly worked out when Lancine met a young woman newly arrived from Africa in 2001. It wasn't entirely chance – a friend who knew one of Madosu's brother suggested a 'meet-up'. And when the two began dating it soon was obvious that sparks were flying.

Still it wasn't always easy for Lancine. He once again had to show his patience and persistence in wooing the woman who would eventually become Mohamed's mother.

"I gave her my phone number right away but she never called. I had to keep trying for a while," he said with a laugh.

Lancine persisted and continued his courtship for almost two years. He quickly learned to use Madosu's nearly two-hour bus trip to her job at a Minneapolis nursing home as an excuse to drive her to and from work daily. The effort didn't go unnoticed by her or her family.

"He became almost a member of the family," she said with a laugh, recalling Lancine's nearly constant presence. "But when he proposed, I was very joyful."

It was a match that has defied some stereotypes of African gender roles. Madosu has continued to be a strong, independent woman while Lancine is clearly the father figure of the family. Both have likely adapted. But Lancine also remembered his father's words in deciding whom his American wife should be.

"My dad always told me that when you get married that beauty is a good thing. But that should not be the goal. A beautiful mind should be the goal," said Lancine. "And he said to watch how she cares about her family. Because if you don't care about your family you will never care about someone else's family."

Incredibly, they would find that they already had a family connection. Madosu's grandmother had been a Fofana – though her home had been far from Guinea. It was yet one more bond they could rely on in difficult times.

"They have a very, very unique relationship. A Guinean man marrying a Liberian woman is very interesting," said close friend, Andrea Cloud, who has lived many years in West Africa and who, incidentally, in 1999 ended up on the sad flight that carried Amadou Diallo's body back to Africa.

Lancine and Madosu's 2003 marriage was only part of the joy that year, as they also learned they were to be parents. In preparation for the life change, Madosu quit her job in the nursing home and set up a hair-braiding business which she still runs out of their home in Brooklyn Park. That was only the beginning of changes, though they had to go through some more suspense for the biggest, er … smallest one.

On January 14 2003, Lancine and Madosu became proud parents of a son who weighed in at 8.6 pounds after being approximately a month overdue. He was named Mohamed, a commonly-used, proud name not only in the Islamic faith but also in the Fofana family. The baby was actually named after one of Lancine's uncles. In his parents' eyes, this latest Mohamed was from the start seen as special and worthy of his name.

"He never slept at night unless you were holding him and looking at him," remembered Madosu with a smile. "We didn't get much sleep. But he was so happy and lovable."

Mohamed was equally the apple of his father's eye, overcoming his late arrival by rapidly growing both physically and mentally.

"He was so smart and learned so fast," said Lancine, recalling with pride that his son started to walk within seven months of age. His precociousness would continue, with both parents laughing as they recalled how as a toddler he learned to turn on the family computer and began typing. Of course at that point Mohamed didn't yet know how to read and write, although she would soon learn to do so in both English and Mandingo.

"He was so curious and loved school. The only complaint we ever got from school was that sometimes he wouldn't go out to play or go to lunch," recalled Lancine of his son. Mohamed even persuaded his parents to allow him to attend two different pre-school programs in the North Minneapolis area while trying to satiate his early love for learning.

Maybe Mohamed just needed to find the right school. That would soon come.

Mohamed's parents, Lancine and Madosu, both left West Africa for Minnesota seeking safety, education and better futures. In Lancine's hometown of Seguiri, Guinea, children and even entire families work dangerous jobs in gold-mining areas where tunnel collapses and environmental risks are part of daily life.

Lancine (left) delivers sports equipment and other supplies to community leaders in Siguiri, Guinea just prior to a soccer game in honor of U.S. visitors and backers of the Mohamad Fofana Memorial School.

The school (above) remains only partially completed. But enthusiasm remains high in the community. Hundreds turned out warmly responding to speeches and ceremonies held under the hot African sun at a nearby soccer field

Chapter 2

"Don't it always seem to go, you don't know what you got til it's gone. They paved paradise, put up a parking lot."
– Joni Mitchell, *Big Yellow Taxi*

It was the summer of 1965 and most of Minnesota focused attention on the Minnesota Twins' drive for their first pennant, American astronauts walking in space or on concerning accounts of war in a place called Vietnam. Meanwhile Huck Finn's life in the tiny riverfront community of Lilly Dale, or Lilydale, was beginning to come to an end.

That spring's massive flooding over the banks of the Mississippi River had driven most residents to higher ground. Layers of mud and debris were pushed up to the roof lines of the town's generally ramshackle houses along the former River Road, as if to mark the hubris of humans in settling on a floodplain. No one was hurt but the devastation was widespread. The surviving 50-60 homes of Lilydale, that included dilapidated trailers, sheds, and outhouses, would require major repairs and were increasingly seen as an eyesore by powers-that-be. That most residents were low-income certainly didn't lessen the momentum to find a permanent solution.

It was the era of "urban renewal," even if Lilydale was anything but urban. Like the nearby West Side River Flats residential area near downtown Saint Paul, which was being bulldozed to make way for an industrial park, the upriver village beside Pickerel Lake and adjacent river bluff areas was being eyed for a complete makeover. What exactly that might be wasn't entirely made clear in general statements calling for Lilydale to return to a "natural state."

That lofty goal still remains unrealized, though State Legislature authorization to make the area into a Regional Park would finally come in 1971. However funding for improvements would be limited for decades.

But after 2008 the availability of Minnesota sales tax Legacy dollars, with portions sliced off for city staff payroll and other costs, would help prompt renewed interest in Lilydale. Saint Paul Parks planners today continue to promote asphalt roadways and buildings in the Mississippi River floodplain area as their interpretation of "natural." Seemingly forgotten, again, is the history of Mother Nature's cycles.

Sadly, similarly forgotten were centuries of Native American trading and hunting patterns throughout the area before European settlement. This despite Lilydale's geographic location approximately midway between the major Dakota community of Kaposia and Pike Island – a place which has long had very special significance as the junction of the Mississippi and Minnesota Rivers. Some suggest it was part of Dakota creation stories long before it was the place where the first fraudulent treaty was signed - a treaty that led to the building of Ft. Snelling and white dominance over the entire Twin Cities area.

About the only history now being preserved in Lilydale is buried under large mounds of earth containing the bulldozed remains of Saint Paul's old West Side Flats. Those low-income immigrant homes and businesses were also forced to make way for "progress" in the mid-1960s. Some former residents moved up the hill, while others scattered along with Lilydale residents whose homes were also buried in the floodplain.

Clearly the area's human and natural sides have long been intertwined - or maybe tangled would be a better description. Historical accounts still haven't resolved whether the small community that peaked at less than 200 people, and an approximately equal number of dogs, was originally spelled with one or two "L's," At root to the Lilly Dale or Lilydale question is whether the Mississippi River town was named for a popular river boatman's song of the mid-19th Century ("Lilly") or for the lily pads that were once prominent in adjacent Pickerel Lake.

Human influence and economic interests would, of course, prevail over the lily pads. Lilydale sprang up as a small, unplanned settlement whose geography and resources shaped its identity. In various ways it became a source of construction materials feeding the growth of Saint Paul and many other cities up and down the river.

First it was a collection and sorting point for huge

collections (rafts) of logs that were floated down the Mississippi. Later the J.L. Shiely Gravel quarry operation would dominate the upstream part of the area. Still later, the Twin Cities Brick Company would carve its mark into the downstream river-bluffs above the town during its nearly 80 years of doing business.

Future Minnesota governor Alexander Ramsey was one of the first major land speculators in Lilydale, as expressed in an 1855 filing. He would graze his cattle in the area along Pickerel Lake for years. Old photos show them on each side of the rail underpass that informally became a roadway and stage coach link from Saint Paul to Mendota. That connection was only possible because of Ramsey's multi-level interest in local real estate.

Ramsey, and other territorial movers and shakers such as Henry Sibley, were primarily interested in railroad opportunities through the Lilydale area. Their Chicago, St. Paul, Minneapolis and Omaha Railroad was incorporated in 1857 and given a federal charter in 1857. Along with it came an exclusive right-of-way and a swing bridge across the Mississippi. The charter's legal power continues in full force today, under the control of the Union Pacific Railroad.

Indeed it has thus far stymied the plans of Saint Paul Parks and Recreation officials wanting to run utilities to their envisioned new park buildings, but requiring railroad permission to use the underpass that was originally Ramsey's old cattle-crossing.

The fog of history can sometimes, but not always, obscure legal distinctions. But there is no doubt Lilydale's familiarity with ambition and scandal began early.

In 1906 there were allegations and indictments against Lily Dale officials for misappropriation of $500 in state funds designated for local roads and bridge repair. The charges were dropped, but the Village incorporation was dissolved and it was returned to the jurisdiction of nearby Mendota for 50 years.

Then in 1951 the Shiely Gravel Company offered the 50 families of Lilydale $5,000 in road improvements if they would again incorporate. Of course it was also understood that they would approve the company's proposal for expansion of its rock quarry. Lily Dale residents indeed lived up to their end of the bargain, approving the plan. Somehow the deal survived a legal challenge from Mendota under the Corrupt Practices Act.

However, the new Village of Lilydale had little time to celebrate its victory and new roads before an April 1952 Mississippi River flood ravaged the area. Most villagers fled on foot to higher ground, although four homeowners needed to rent a barge to have their property taken downriver to safety. For most however, mobile trailer homes that sprang up around Lilydale became the favored response to Mother Nature.

Her temptations were tough to resist no matter how clear her rejections. The river valley beauty was an obvious attraction. But it was the quieter aspects of the lifestyle that kept most of its residents there despite floods, along with poverty and other hardships. Nostalgia for the semi-rural, libertarian atmosphere pervades the stories of those remembering life on the Huck Finn frontier.

"As a kid there, I built a raft and spent the first half of my day fishing in the river and the second half I went swimming in Pickerel Lake," recalled John Darlow, who grew up in Lilydale from 1955 to 1965 and for decades remained nearby as owner of the River Road Bait Shop. "I can't even explain what it was like, it was so beautiful. ...Sure, we were poor. But it was like the Flats, we all knew each other and got along."

The story is repeated many times over among those who grew up in or around Lilydale before the 1965 diaspora.

"It was great for us kids. The fishing was great in Pickerel and in the winter the Certified Ice Company would come and cut ice out of the lake. That was exciting," said Mike Mrozinski, who was born in Lilydale in 1926 and whose mother lived there through the 1960s. His father was one of the last commercial fishermen on that stretch of the Mississippi.

Time, of course, helps erase painful memories. But former Lilydale residents almost universally have focused on the area's idyllic childhood opportunities.

"If every kid could have grown up like we did down there. ...It was Tom Sawyer every day," recalled Ed Peltier, who with his brother Phil grew up near the intersection of Water and Joy streets from 1933 to 1952. Fishing and swimming were also part of their daily lives, along with climbing in and out of caves carved into the river-bluffs or hunting for fossils that seemed to wash downhill after each rainfall.

Lilydale wasn't yet widely known as a Midwest mecca for fossil-hunting of petrified fish and other creatures from a pre-historic period. However, as the Twin Cities Brick Company cut deeply into river-bluffs to extract materials it also increasingly uncovered more and more delights for youngsters.

These children were almost all white and local. But the appeal of the area was universal long before Mohamed was born.

"For us kids there was that lure of water and woods. There was always something to do. We were real river rats," said Peltier.

Even the "hill rats" who either walked down stairs located beside the High Bridge, or otherwise found their way down from Cherokee Heights, reveled in the attractions of the Lilydale area. A favorite pastime of West Side and Lilydale youth was to "moon" passengers on the Mankato-bound train that regularly passed by their Pickerel Lake swimming hole.

"We used to stand on the bridge and wait 'til the engineer would blow the whistle before we'd jump in," remembered Bill Meehn, a teenager in the late 1930s. "And the only suits we had on were our birthday suits."

Lilydale during that era had plenty of attractions for neighborhood kids even in cooler weather, with the brickyard kilns always warming things up.

"We'd come down through the Ivy Falls (then known as "Happy Hollow") for a shower," recalled Wayne Schmidt of Mendota Heights. "Then when we were done we'd go and dry off at the brickyards."

Others would come down to camp on "Dead Man's Hill" overlooking Pickerel Lake – never dreaming of the tragedy that would decades later mark a nearby part of the river-bluff area.

"We were mostly worried about the railroad Hobo Jungle near there," recounted Mike Kluznik of times in the early 1950s. "I don't think there was really that much worry but we kept our fire going all night, cooking frog legs, and we had crazy plans to defend ourselves by rolling burning logs down at what we called the bums and maniacs."

Mostly the boys just played in the woods and weeds all day.

"It did harken back to Huck Finn and Tom Sawyer," concluded Kluznik. "Course it's probably good we didn't stay out there longer or it might have been more like Lord of the Flies."

Life wasn't always so easy in Lilydale for those with adult worries. It's population lived an often hard-scrabble life, literally struggling to keep their heads above water. Between floods, a shortage of plumbing and other hardships. This version of the American dream didn't involve any McMansions or happy Hollywood endings.

"We were all pretty poor people. There were no wealthy neighbors. "...Course we were pretty spread apart," Mrozinski said of the semi-rural community. Lilydale residents had to generally be self-reliant.

"It was tough. I went to bed hungry at night lots of times," recalled Bob Hammond, who grew up as a third-generation Lilydaler in the 1920s. "I remember my grandfather had a herd of cattle and there were loggers around and people did just about anything. ...Course most of us were squatters. We never paid taxes back then."

Lilydale residents made a living anyway they could, including growing mushrooms or making cheese in caves, raising cows and chickens, and even operating a pig farm, among other ventures. It was conveniently located near a dumping grounds for the "slop" wagon, which regularly traveled the nearby West Side picking up household food scraps and other garbage.

But the main source of employment was the Twin Cities Brick Company, founded in 1894. The company offered steady work for decades to those willing to do a variety of manual labor.

Many locals worked outside year-round pulling clay and limestone out of the river bluffs - usually by hand. Material mined from limestone found in the hillside would turn into millions of bricks. Some bricks called for an additional mix with St. Peter sandstone which was also found in abundance just below the limestone.

All the material was mined, usually by shovel, and carried down the steep slope via a conveyor belt system. There at a mill it was mixed, molded and sliced off into bricks to be piled on carts by workers. Rusted iron remnants of the conveyor belt system can still be seen in Lilydale Park today.

Other Lilydalers would operate the nearby six or eight kilns that heated up to 900 degrees. The ovens were originally fired by coal and later by oil burners. Bricks were fired to a white-hot temperature for up to a week. After being fired they would slowly cool nearby on a concrete area until workers could stack them in preparation for transport.

Local workers would then load pallets onto trucks that motored up the hill on a narrow trail. But more shipments would take advantage of the railway spur line that ran along Pickerel Lake past a brick office building and a couple of boarding houses. In the office, there was a display area where prospective buyers could be shown different styles of bricks.

The sales pitch was effective for decades. Bricks from Lilydale would be part of structures throughout the entire upper Mississippi Valley watershed, including the nearby downtown Saint Paul Hotel and faraway Saskatchewan buildings. They were the basis of a major legal action in 1913 that saw the Twin Cities Brick Company win an almost unheard of victory against the railroad for its over-pricing of rates applied to carrying bricks to Duluth.

Evidence of brickyard history still remains in three quarry areas known as the East, Middle, and West Clay Pits and in the ruins of one brick kiln. Near the oven remains is Echo Cave, a man-made feature used for storage but now barred-up to protect an endangered bat species that has come to make its home there. The entire cave was originally carved into white Cambrian sandstone rock. That bluff material was also valued in the early 1900s for its high silica content used to make glass in bottles used for breweries that popped up all over the West Side and West End neighborhoods of Saint Paul.

Alcohol certainly was a part of Lilydale life. At times the secluded community had a somewhat seedy reputation. During Prohibition, the "Mystic Caverns" (man-made caves built into the bluff-side) were widely known as a beer-and-booze-lovers hideaway. A dance hall and bar near the Omaha Bridge was a hot-spot well into the 1950s. In the next decade, the town was known for its automobile salvage yards and a Bohemian lifestyle in a riverfront marina community that sometimes involved a variety of mind-altering substances.

But if life was rough-and-tumble, the residents of Lilydale seemed to generally pull together – or at least practice a high level of tolerance for each other.

"It was quite a quaint little community. Everybody knew everybody. If somebody got too out of line they'd give 'em a kick without having to worry about their parents calling a lawyer," said Peltier. "They were good old days."

But they were inevitably coming to an end. The 1965 flood was a back-breaker for the old Lilydale. Nearly every home was flooded at least up to the first floor and many were simply washed away from their foundations. Streets were almost washed away, with sewer run-off and garbage strewn everywhere. Water-borne illnesses were a major concern with every flood.

"It was really a mess. I pitied anybody going back into that," recalled former West Sider Tom Mahoney, who as a telephone company employee at the time was one of the first people to re-enter Lilydale. "A lot of people had already decided they'd had enough."

The Twin Cities Brick Company was also on its last legs, with declining sales. It would finally close in 1972 with nearly all buildings razed five years later. But its footprint still remains in the gouged out hillsides that would continue to be the source of fossil-hunting delight - and ultimately tragedy.

Some were happy to take a small government buyout for their property. But for many, being forced to move from the area was an injustice never to be forgotten.

"Most of the people felt it was worth it just to live in a beautiful place like that. ...People loved that place, floods or no floods," Darlow said. "The people on this side of the river were a different breed."

Yet Ramsey and Dakota County officials decided it was time to turn Lilydale to better use as part of new regional park. It took several years to complete eminent domain condemnation proceedings and settle lawsuits from unhappy residents. Marina owner Wayne Brown and one other elderly homeowner were allowed to remain on leases until the early 1980s. But the long arm of the law would eventually succeed against all who had fought off Mother Nature for so many years.

In 1983, jurisdiction over the 384-acre Lilydale Park was officially given to the City of Saint Paul in a curious land swap. Most of the area is actually in a separate (Dakota) county and municipality (the newly created City of Lilydale.) But the park was first castoff to Ramsey County. Then the city agreed to take over operational control in exchange for Ramsey County gaining control of Battle Creek and Pigs Eye Lake areas.

Yet, after the trade, the city appeared to lose interest in Lilydale Park. Not until 1991 did Saint Paul Parks & Recreation adopt a theoretical "Master Plan" for the area.

It included ambitious concepts such as a trailer park, swimming beach etc. that proved to be both unfeasible and unpopular with Lilydale's limited number of users. Few city resources would be spent on the area. A general laissez faire attitude continued for decades with minimal attention from city Parks staff - except to continue giving out fossil-hunting permits.

Meanwhile Mother Nature made a return of sorts, including in areas most scarred by the Twin Cities Brick Company. Fast-growing trees and grasses filled in many gaps. Wildlife and Mississippi River Flyway fowl returned as Lilydale's main inhabitants. Former brickyard roads became great informal hiking trails for local youth, dog-walkers, fossil-hunters and others.

But the area also attracted garbage dumpers along roadsides and into the waters of Pickerel Lake. Tires and abandoned cars would years later be dragged out by neighborhood activists and fishermen. Vagrants, though generally harmless, set up tents or camps in secluded areas. Youth would break into barred-off caves and occasionally become trapped. Lilydale was increasingly a no-man's land getting a reputation among some as a dangerous place.

Into this void of any serious governmental interest, The Friends of Lilydale Park (FOL) was born in 1999.

We were officially an offshoot of the West Side Citizens Organization (WSCO) but never had any paid staff or funding. More ad hoc than organized, our volunteers would string together bird and nature hikes, history programs, family fishing outings, fossil hunts, and a variety of year-round programs for the next 15 years. Our participants came from Saint Paul neighborhoods and surrounding suburban areas and beyond. The only criteria for involvement was appreciation for Lilydale Park.

FOL included characters such as Cliff Timm, an aging angler who would endlessly lobby friend and foe alike on the worthy goal of promoting water quality and fishing in Pickerel Lake. His initial goal was a levee protecting it from Mississippi River floodwaters. But as legal and other barriers to that questionable idea grew, he generously moved on to providing fishing piers, free fishing rods and gear for low-income youth from the area. Eventually he threw himself energetically into eliminatingCanadian geese and their excrement from the area.

FOL cleanups of the lake, trails and adjacent areas soon led to other projects such as butterfly habitat development utilizing milkweed native to the area. Volunteers would weekly spend time counting and documenting Monarch eggs and larvae, along with other evidence of annual migration from Mexico and other points south. Volunteers planted seeds for wildflower gardens alongside a new lakeside boat ramp for canoes and kayaks for which FOL helped fundraise.

We really hit our stride with a project in 2001 to create a trail and overlook high on the bluffs above the park.

Partnering with a small national environmental organization and fundraiser/lead organizer, James Mallman, Vento's View was hacked out of scrub-trees and the use of Kasota stone rock that had originally been part of the first St. Paul City Hall/Courthouse in the 19th century. The giant stones were returned to river bluff origins in the shape of an amphitheater that made for sweeping vistas of the entire park and Mississippi River valley.

The project's completion came in on-budget and time thanks to donated funds and labor. Parks officials who at first seemed reluctant, or perhaps uncertain what to make of citizen groups bearing gifts, eventually acquiesced to our entreaties. Our anticipated grand-opening was scheduled in time for a national environmental conference in Saint Paul – on September 11, 2001.

Needless to say, there was a delay in the dedication of Vento's View, named for recently-deceased former Saint Paul Congressman Bruce Vento. But when the event finally happened a couple weeks later all went perfectly - until the Congressman's attending relatives became involved in an imbroglio over inheritance issues. It ended with a pair of brothers fighting and rolling on the ground along the new trail until police arrived.

Friends of Lilydale, however, generally continued to enjoy peaceful relations with its neighbors and City Hall during this time. In fact, our ragtag group was successful on a number of fronts in raising the visibility of Lilydale

Park and making incremental improvements aimed at improving human access to the area while protecting its unique natural features.

Our next major effort was to lead the drive, including raising all funds, to create a safe, stable, unpaved trail from the top of the river bluff to the bottom. We found sponsors for interpretive signage and later added benches along the mile-and-a-half Brickyard Trail. Increasing numbers of users could now more easily sample the park's rugged offerings and learn of its history. Trail and park users included increasing numbers of school groups regularly having classes at Vento's View amphitheater before walking down the trail to safely access fossil areas.

In 2003, at the request of Saint Paul Parks & Recreation planner Tim Agnes, a fence was added around the overlook, restricting access to the bluffside. It was specifically intended to address safety concerns about clearly visibly crumbling bluff edges – as was typical in Lilydale Park.

Next on the FOL list in 2009 was development of an urban youth camping program in the park, which previously had no legal overnight guests. We secured a sizable camping equipment grant from REI for tents and other items and then held several test events. A number of inner-city young people had their first experiences in Lilydale with campfire-making, canoeing and kayaking on a lake and seeing wildlife. That some of the wildlife unfortunately involved drunken partiers in a parking lot was only a minor issue – aside from the disturbing inability of police dispatchers to find Lilydale Park on the map. That incident was witnessed by a Parks staffer who with us during the outing.

Our efforts gained attention in local media, including a 2004 *St. Paul Pioneer Press* article in which city Parks Director Bob Bierscheid praised Friends of Lilydale as "emblematic of lots of groups in Saint Paul that are critical to our work ... they are willing to put their time and energy where their mouths are."

Honors continued with myself and my wife, Grit Youngquist, each being named Park Citizens of the Year at different times in the mid-2000s. Then in 2008, FOL was given the city's first ever Citizens Group of the Year award. Mayor Chris Coleman, who lives near the park and would occasionally jog the Brickyard Trail, presented the honor and posed with us for pictures.

It was the beginning of the end.

Things began to change just a few months later when Coleman appointed Mike Hahm to replace the retiring, community-minded Bierscheid as director of Saint Paul Parks and Recreation. The brusque, bald-headed Hahm - whom some would come to compare to Lex Luthor – had previously headed up the city's popular, highly-developed Como Park that couldn't have been more different from Lilydale's wild, untamed nature. His approach and skills were perhaps better focused on keeping trains running on time.

In fairness, ever-increasing financial pressures on the Park system, as state budget cuts trickled down, had a variety of impacts. Maintenance costs, new programs and projects that weren't visibly popular or couldn't pay for themselves were going to be increasingly difficult to justify.   Finding new sources of revenue was an understandable concern.

But Parks project priorities began to seem based largely on what would bring in big dollar grants. Especially attractive were the Met Council and the Minnesota Legacy sales tax funds, from which slices could be taken to pay for Park's planners' / designers' billable time. Bricks and mortar projects were the easiest for justifying large budgets. At times it appeared Parks had almost gone into the construction business, with projects including asphalt roads and asphalt paths, as its new central function.

We increasingly started hearing from Parks planners that they no longer had funding to justify attending community meetings. Yet, pressure subtly mounted to build a new $5 million roadway along with parking lots in Lilydale Park, to be followed later by picnic pavilions. At one point Parks staff planned to build across several wetlands areas until we pointed it out to Army Corps of Engineer officials.

But it was a temporary victory. The plan was allowed to go ahead after St. Paul agreed to pay tax dollars into a "wetland bank" generally used to subsidize wetlands development outstate or in suburban office park areas.

Increasingly secondary to the city were FOL priorities focused on restoring Lilydale as a natural oasis in an urban area. We favored relatively low-cost, low-impact projects such as nature trail development, interpretive signage and other protections of Lilydale's environmentally endangered areas.

The shift in emphasis was evident in Park's reaction to their consultant's 2009 report on Lilydale's natural resources. The analysis described the dangerously eroding bluff line as a top concern, along with related pollution of Pickerel Lake. It called for a full study of storm-water ravines and the carved-out walls of old Twin Cities Brick Company clay pit areas throughout the park.

The natural resources study affirmed concerns of community members who had noted landslides at Vento's View and elsewhere. We again brought up the report's recommendation for further analysis of the erosion problem at a public hearing. The study would have cost $12,000-15,000. But Saint Paul Parks & Recreation claimed it didn't have the money even as it continued plans for another new $2.5 million roadway and asphalt trail just above Lilydale in Cherokee Park.

Interestingly, during the same time period a similar ravine erosion issue in Saint Paul's more prosperous Highland Park area did receive nearly $15,000 in funding to look at stabilization options. Staff person Mike Kimble in 2011 drafted a policy for handling storm-water in parks that he forwarded to the department's lead planner, Jody Martinez.

"I think it's sure a good idea worth pursueing, (sic)" she responded. But there is no further record of any storm-water plan ever being developed or implemented.

Meanwhile the Lilydale Park bluff was deteriorating in increasingly visible ways. In late April 2011 a giant collapse took down almost an entire hillside known as the North Knob, just 50 yards away from the ravine where Mohamed and Haysem Sani would be killed two years later.

This time everyone was lucky. The so-called North Knob landslide happened very late at night, especially fortuitous since the area had been known for decades as a drinking hangout for area teens. But no one was hurt and no private property was threatened, though Lilydale Park was dramatically changed for all to see. The trees, rocks and mud slide part way down the bluff created a temporary swimming hole of sorts. It was used for several weeks by local kids. But the accumulation of storm-water still coming down the hill eventually caused the ad hoc dam to give away – again mercifully during the night.

That 2011 mudslide was definitely noticed by multiple community residents and Saint Paul Parks employees. A scheduled nature hike in the area later that summer had to be canceled with the city staffer taking a photo of the foot-deep mud that had oozed all the way down the hillside nearly a mile away. I personally showed and described the slide to several city employees.

Email exchanges between a National Park Service employee, alerted by a citizen, and Parks supervisor Cy Kosel led him to send out his own alert to key people in the department.

"Another landslide? We should check out to see if it is creating other issues," wrote Kosel in an email that investigators would later include, without comment, in their report on the 2013 tragedy.

There were however no actions or precautions taken by Parks staff following the 2011 incident. Their much ballyhooed Great River Passages plan, approved in 2012, did call for $500,000 in bluff-top storm-water treatment projects throughout the Mississippi River valley and included a map of Cherokee Park bluff problem areas. But no action was taken to implement the advertised plan or to bring public attention to potential safety issues.

Lilydale Park's bluff areas continued to remain open to neighborhood kids who climbed the hillsides, innocently looking for fun in all its hidden corners. School groups like the Peter Hobart Elementary students who would continue to come looking for fossils would still regularly explore nearby ravines. Lilydale was seemingly reverting to something like the children's paradise old timers remembered.

"Kids need that. I had it and I still remember," said John Darlow, though adding an ominous premonition. "But it will never come again like it was."

He was right. Lilydale would soon again become Paradise Lost in its most tragic fashion yet.

Village of Lilydale, 1939

Paradise lost or found?

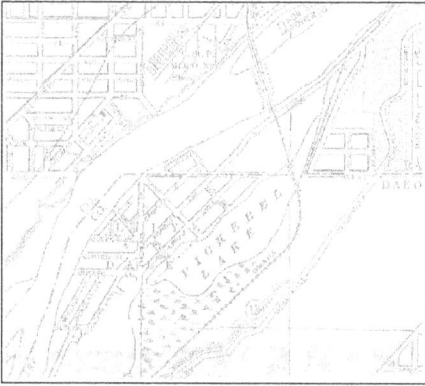

Lilydale was born at the intersection of Mississippi River and railroad interests in the mid-19th century. It grew into a company town dominated by the Twin Brickyard Company & the legacy of Huck Finn.

The natural world, including swimming & fishing in Pickerel Lake, was a part of daily life even as the brickyards operation carved into the bluffsides. But it was river flooding that led to the town's demise in the 1960's.

Lilydale Park suffered nearly 30 years of neglect until neighborhood advocates stepped in. Friends of Lilydale and city officials at first worked together to open trails & nature programs. But alas, Parks planners were more interested in monuments, buildings and roads.

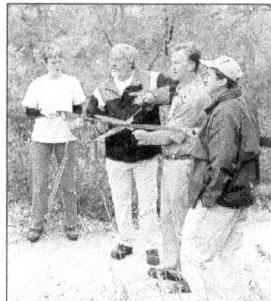

human impacts on Lilydale Park were evident when Saint Paul took over control in 1983. Sludge piles (below) and unstable cliffs were apparent to a Parks & Recreation staffer in 2004 when he ordered a cast iron fence around Vento's View (right.) A 2009 consultant's report (bottom left) called on the city to do a full study of storm-water and other erosion of blufflines. Impacts from a 2011 landslide (bottom right), including mud flows over half a mile away, were witnessed by Parks staff.

Lilydale Regional Park - Saint Paul, Minnesota

Lilydale Regional Park
Fossil Ground

Water & Joy streets former intersection & parking lot where first responders were sent, far downhill from accident site.

May 22, 2013 landslide location where Peter Hobart students hunt fossils

City culvert un-plugging project sending storm-water under road into Lilydale Park accident site

Brickyard Trail gate - nearest & best emergency access point & location of 911 calls.

Chapter 3

"The Koran says that when a good person dies, the angels come to retrieve the soul and escort it to heaven."

--Kadiatou Diallo, *My Heart Will Cross This Ocean: My Story, My Son Amadou*

Mohamed Fofana awoke on May 22, 2013 excitedly looking forward to a special day in his young life. Like others in his 4th grade class at Peter Hobart Elementary in St. Louis Park, he was going on a field trip to a new place looking for remnants of a time gone by. It was a place where one could dream of dinosaurs, pre-historic sharks and other creatures.

"He was so excited when he told me he was going on a field trip to look for fossils. I'd never heard of Lilydale Park and I said, 'What?" recalled Mohamed's father, Lancine. "But he was really looking forward to it. The whole night before he was talking about it and getting ready to go. He didn't care if it might be raining or not. He wanted to go so bad."

Fossil-hunting has been part of Lilydale for many decades. It attracted locals and visitors from long distances who had learned of the opportunities that the Twin City Brick Company's excavations had opened. For the most part, fossil-hunting was usually a low-key, informal activity with only an occasional sprained ankle off-setting generations of fun, family-friendly visits.

Hints of future calamity were occasionally there, along with the past. In 1953 a visiting geologist from Illinois was killed by a slab of limestone falling from a bluff top.

But Lilydale's generally safe fossil hunting really began to take off in the 1980s after it became a Metropolitan Regional Park. Institutions including the Science Museum of Minnesota, the University of Minnesota, local geological groups and numerous school groups came to the park from throughout the Twin Cities area, and even further. Visitors virtually had the run of the place. Thousands of young people got introductions to fossil hunting over the years. While Saint Paul Parks & Recreation officially required permits, there were few restrictions and almost no supervision of activities beyond that provided by fossil-hunt group leaders.

Often it was possible to walk through most of Lilydale Park and experience its raw beauty without seeing another human being. Its rough trails, virtually all ad hoc and trampled down by local teenagers, homeless campers or deer - except for those FOL had recently created - led to anywhere and nowhere. Some naturally meandered along creek beds and into deserted, small clay pit areas carved out by the Twin Cities Brick Company.

Of course, it was the very instability of Lilydale's bluffs

that helped make the area such a fossil-lover's attraction. Every rain would uncover new buried treasures from a strange geologic period called the Ordovician Period about 450 million years ago when most of southeastern Minnesota was submerged by a warm, shallow sea. That marine environment is what left behind generally small fossils known as Bryozoans, Brachiopods and Crinoids. Though diminutive, Lilydale fossils are especially beloved by children for their complete patterns and because they are easy to find as they wash down from the park's sandstone bluffs.

The Lilydale brickyards area is made up of mostly St. Peter sandstone, limestone and Decorah shale - all sedimentary rocks that were once part of the old sea bottom. These sliced-open layers of limestone and shale can become especially unstable with the flow and pressure of storm-water on them. Many locals knew to stay away from the top or bottom of bluff edges during or after rains. FOL did its best to regularly caution park visitors we would encounter in Lilydale.

Mohamed and his fellow students and teachers, however, had little or no idea of any danger as they boarded buses to Lilydale Park that morning. There was a light rain, which had actually let up from heavier, soaking downpours of the previous days. Spirits were high with skies beginning to lighten during the 35-minute trip from the St. Louis Park school. Two classes totaling 49 children were supervised on the field trip by two teachers, two para-professionals, seven adult chaperones and a paleontology guide.

Their school buses arrived just after noon. They came through downtown Saint Paul, crossing the Mississippi River to Harriet Island – a river location that was filled in on one side and joined to the West Side neighborhood in the 1920s. Driving down Water Street under what is known as the High Bridge, the buses went about another half mile to an unmarked turnoff onto what 40 years earlier was called Joy Street. The now dead-end, unpaved, potholed area was known to locals and on Parks and Recreation maps simply as the Brickyards parking lot.

There students, teachers and chaperones unloaded for the day's activities in Lilydale Park. It would begin with a muddy walk of approximately three-quarters of a mile on the mostly wooded Brickyards Trail. En route would be a view of Pickerel Lake, the barred-over entrance to Echo Cave and the remains of an old kiln used to fire bricks. Then they marched up the steep-pitched hillside toward fossil-hunting areas.

It was a strenuous uphill hike before reaching what was known as the Middle Clay Pit area. Another, shorter route would have been to enter at the top of the Brickyard Trail from Cherokee Park at the corner of Minnesota Hwy. 13. There was an even nearer gate in a chain-linked fence off Minnesota Hwy. 13, but it was routinely padlocked. While that entrance was also near the main route to the aforementioned Vento's View – a spectacular overlook popular with locals - it was not promoted by Parks officials as an entry point for fossil hunting.

The Peter Hobart students began to spread out over the hillsides, with adults nearby, looking for fossils. Some stuck to more open, accessible areas while others explored further up a creek where water flowed down from the bluffs into what is known as the East Clay Pit.

A number of students, including Mohamed, began exploring the horseshoe shaped canyon area, some 20-40 feet wide at the base of the bluff that had been formed by Brickyard mining. Its carved-out steep sides consisting of layered Decorah shale and sandstone, dropped 30-40 feet from the tree and brush-lined edge above. Recently fallen rocks, washed down by a small waterfall, may have appeared to offer plentiful fossil hunting opportunities.

There was a photo, taken by chaperone Shane Boettcher, of a group of 18 fossil hunters who had moved close to the narrow canyon's walls. The shot, which also included fourth grade teacher Sarah Reichart, was full of young, enthusiastic faces clearly involved and looking forward to that day's discoveries in Lilydale Park.

It was just a few minutes later - about 1:15 in the afternoon – that everything suddenly changed for the Peter Hobart students and staff.

Several accounts described a very loud bang or thunderous boom – like a cannon shot, according to one student. Another described it as sounding like a freight train. One 911 caller said that "a wall had collapsed," an apparent reference to the steeply-sided canyon face.

"We were like, 'What/'" remembered then Saint Paul Fire Department Deputy Chief Matt Simpson of that first-hand account which was itself buried by later media descriptions using more familiar terms like "mudslide" or "saturated slope."

Regardless, it was a massive amount of rock and sand that suddenly came down upon the unsuspecting fossil-hunters. Trees began to snap and topple over into the ravine. Human shouts and screams followed as the tons of earth and timber took both students and adults by surprise.

Those who could run quickly stampeded out of the small, enclosed area. Others were temporarily pinned back further into the canyon before they could scramble out over the now giant pile of rubble partially blocking the entrance.

A few of the group, including Mohamed, were not able to do either. He had disappeared in a moment while others a few feet away were able to leave unscathed. The hillside that had once looked like such a promising source of educational fun had, in a moment, become a source of malevolent education in life, death and fate.

"If my daughter had been any closer, it's hard for me to think and talk about," said parent Andraya Lund of 10-year-old Bella. "She had just followed a couple of guys back in there and was yelling at them to come back when everything came down. They had to pull her leg out of the mess, she tore her pants and lost her shoe. It was very scary. But she was one of the lucky ones."

Mohamed likely never had a chance to escape.

According to some children, he had paused in flight to push two students ahead of him, possibly saving at least one life. It is impossible to know the what really happened. But it was the type of selfless act that his family was used to seeing from him. This time it would be the ultimate sacrifice, though it would not be realized for some time amidst the noise, chaos and dust.

Confusion and shock were understandable immediate reactions. Students and adults alike were momentarily stunned by the unexpected, and continuing, deluge of rock and sand. Those who scrambled away were naturally focused on self-preservation as their first instinct.

Their cries and yells quickly brought the rest of the field trip and leaders running, including fellow fourth grade teacher Penny Dupris. They jumped into action with remarkable speed and calm, helping those at the scene who were digging themselves out. It was a response that likely saved at least one life.

But the giant pile of rock and sand, with still more continuing to slide down bluff side, made rescue efforts of missing students nearly impossible. They had no tools. Even worse, they couldn't be certain how many or exactly where unfortunate members of the Peter Hobart group might be buried. The teachers knew they needed to act quickly.

Reichart was the first to call 911. Without time to do a count of students, she understandably feared the worst.

"We've fallen down an avalanche, and we're, we need an ambulance. We need emergency personnel for about 20 kids," she told the emergency dispatcher. "I don't know how many are buried."

It was a conversation that quickly grew even more confused as Reichart described the school group's name and location in the fossil grounds to a dispatcher who clearly had no familiarity with Lilydale Park.

"Okay, are you by the pavilion?" asked the 911 operator, obviously unaware there was no pavilion - or for that matter any human-made structure - in this particular Saint Paul park. "What's the closest um, ah site that you can see, like ah, like a monument or anything like that?"

Remarkably, Reichart appears in the transcripst to have kept her cool in response. Even while on the telephone, she began taking charge of the first rescue operation – having spotted the familiar long hair of a Peter Hobart fourth grader who was buried under the rubble. With her bare hands she and others, including Boettcher, began trying to dig him out. It was a task made harder by sand and rocks that kept sliding down the hillside.

"Stay calm Devin," Reichart told 10 year-old Devin Meldahl, who was initially covered in sand over his head and struggled to breathe. "Devin, you're alive. You're fine. Devin, you're fine. I got you Devin."

The listening dispatcher tried to offer verbal support.

However, there continued to be a gap in understanding how best to get rescuers to the site. Reichart accurately described how the group had gotten to their hillside location, walking up the switchback Brickyard Trail nearly a mile from the parking lot at Joy and Water streets. But the location-sharing effort was in vain.

"You went straight towards the river?" asked the well-meaning but bewildered dispatcher.

Confusion continued with questions about whether the fossil-hunting group were by an (unnamed) bridge, perhaps referring to either the High Bridge or Wabasha Street Bridge several miles away.

Reichart, who was meanwhile trying to direct school children to places of safety away from the scene and also to get a complete count of the group, decided to try a different tack. She asked the dispatcher to call Peter Hobart Elementary in St. Louis Park and get clear directions to the fossil grounds.

Then Reichart decided to leave Devin's digging out to Boettcher and others. She let the dispatcher know she was going towards what she correctly believed was the closest access location for rescuers.

"Okay go, go to the parking lot. Can you make it to the parking lot?" asked the dispatcher, still referring to Water and Joy streets down the hill nearly a mile away where first emergency units had already been mistakenly sent. Audio tapes would confirm the confusion and frustration those units also faced.

"No, the parking lot is too slow," responded Reichart, correctly. "I'm gonna go up to Cherokee Heights and Annapolis Street, it's way closest."

Adrenaline had clearly kicked in as she began running up the steep Brickyard Trail, roughly 200 yards from Highway 13 (Annapolis Street) with a metal gate entrance in a chain-link fence. Sirens could be heard as the teacher climbed the hill. It must have appeared that help was nearly there.

But again there was confusion as emergency vehicles and teams at first went racing by. They were headed several hundred yards to the east to the Cherokee Boulevard entrance to Lilydale Park.

Reichart's exasperation obviously grew even as she came closer to the top of the hill where she believed help awaited. The dispatcher told her to stay on the line.

"I'm staying. I can hear them coming. Oh my god. I think they are going away from where, where I am," she said to the 911 official.

The back-and-forth continued for several minutes as the dispatcher again talked about responders arriving at the corner of Joy and Water streets. Apparently sensing the telephone caller's dismay, the Ramsey County employee urged Reichart to slow down and avoid a medical situation herself.

"I just can't believe this happened," responded Reichart. "I can hear sirens, tell them I'm at the old gate where they have it chained and I'm up at Cherokee Heights. ... I'm standing in front of a house."

The Peter Hobart field trip leader had actually arrived at the locked Highway 13 gate. It was just a few hundred yards from Cherokee Boulevard but far enough away to confuse the dispatcher now trying to locate non-existent house numbers on the wrong street.

"I'm at the gate where the fence is chained," said Reichart, trying again to describe the situation. "Good God. I can hear them but I can't get to them. They seem to be stopping ahead of me. Tell them they got to stop there and walk behind the fence to me. They'll be to me on that path but I can't reach. ... I can't get out. I'm trapped in the park behind a chained fence."

"God damn it," responded the understandably exasperated dispatcher at one point, who obviously knew little about Lilydale Park, but was sincerely trying to understand where exactly to send emergency vehicles.

"Tell them to stop! Hello! Hello! Hello! I'm here! I got them," said Reichart, who finally had succeeded in waving down Saint Paul Fire Department personnel. "Can you break this chain! Can you break this chain and come in this way?"

Captain Paul Barrett was one of the first responders on site, sent from downtown Saint Paul along with a ladder truck almost as an after-thought despite his training as a medic.

"It didn't come in to us like a serious call at first," he said, remembering that he asked his supervisor if he might go along. "We didn't know if it was somebody fell off a cliff or got stuck somewhere or what."

Some first reports mistakenly described students walking on a trail or rain-soaked bluff that gave way underneath them. It almost sounded as if it were a quick-sand-like situation. Again, 911 dispatchers and emergency personnel were clearly unfamiliar with Lilydale Park geography, landscapes and dangers.

Not that Barrett and other Saint Paul first responders weren't very serious about their rescue responsibilities, especially once they got a grasp of the situation. There was ultimately no shortage of resources devoted to efforts to save all the Peter Hobart fossil-hunting group. Five crews and a District Chief were sent out along with large numbers of other support personnel. Eventually there would be a total of 21 agencies involved, all responding with urgency, even if delayed by the initial 911 befuddlement.

After Barrett and his team followed Reichart and other

Peter Hobart adult leaders to the landslide site, they quickly saw how serious things were. Devin Meldahl still remained partially buried in the rock and sand. Teachers had now done a count and realized that at least three students were missing, including Mohamed. One student, Lucas Lee, was found a short time later, suffering from relatively mild physical injuries but, like so many there, facing serious emotional impact.

First responders, including Barrett, recognized they were working against time in a hazardous situation. Uninjured students and teachers from Peter Hobart were immediately moved away from the ravine. Emergency personnel literally dove into action, urgently working to dig Devin out by hand while rocks continued to fall from the bluff wall. Two firefighters later required their own medical attention.

The slippery terrain also created problems, with one police officer having to be lowered by her belt into the hole where Devin was partially buried so that she could dig by hand.

Shovels and other necessary tools had not been indicated as a need in early dispatches. Some emergency crews at the top of the bluffs began throwing tools over the edge, while police officers were sent out to Cherokee Park neighborhood houses seeking implements. One newspaper account described a local landscaper having his truck and equipment temporarily commandeered by desperate rescue personnel. Police reports indicated that officers eventually brought shovels from locations in Saint Paul as far away as Como High School.

The effort to save Devin soon revealed an even more desperate situation.

Barrett remembered being sprawled across a still-shifting pile of debris, helping to dig out Meldahl's leg, when he suddenly struck something else in the sand. It was a human hand. They frantically dug down to find the head of another victim, Haysem Sani. The nine-year-old, also the son of an African immigrant family, had been completely buried by several feet of rock and sand.

It was quickly assessed that Mohamed was likely also buried in the area. Rescue personnel jumped in almost on top of each other in the limited space, heroically trying to extricate both of the victims - beginning with Haysem. Eventually there would actually be too many fire, police, parks workers and others at the site, all wanting to help.

"Our biggest concern when we arrived was the lack of coordination," said Deputy Fire Chief Jim Smith, who had also been delayed by going to the Water & Joy address before climbing up the hill. "It was like herding cats to get people out of there at first."

The first responders soon were organized into groups of five, relieving each other every ten minutes as diggers became fatigued. They were battling more rocks and sand falling from the bluff, as well as the clock.

It was soon apparent that given the lengthy amount of

time which had passed since the original landslide that their efforts were in vain. A decision was made to focus first on Meldahl before the situation might become more dangerous, and potentially fatal, for all still in the ravine.

"It was heartbreaking," recalled Barrett. "There were grown men crying. Nobody ever wants to see a kid die. We just couldn't do anything. It was so frustrating, but we had to go on."

The mix of first responders did finish digging out Devin fairly quickly, and then strapped him into an airlift gurney. A helicopter line was dropped into the ravine area and he was delivered to a waiting ambulance to be taken to Regions Hospital.

His injuries, both physical and emotional, would be serious but not life-threatening. Devin would be found to have sustained an orbital eye fracture, a total of eight fractured ribs, collapsed lungs, multiple breaks in his legs and an assortment of other serious bumps and bruises.

The noise of helicopters in the area would be a continuing fixture throughout the rest of the day and long into the evening. A combination of hospital medivac, state and local police search-and-rescue and media aircraft were constantly buzzing over Lilydale Park and the West Side neighborhood. Local TV and radio broadcasters soon arrived to begin ongoing live updates on the situation.

As attention turned back to unearthing Haysem and finding any other possible victims, it became apparent that the situation was becoming ever more treacherous for everyone. One firefighter had been struck on the head by a rock and the left sidewall of the canyon continued to slough off substantial amounts of sand and rock.

While generally only misting rain throughout the day, Deputy Fire Chief Smith's report described the volume of water flowing off the cliff increasing into a small stream running through the site. Only later would the source of all the storm-water that poured over the bluff and down into the ravine come into question.

Smith had other more immediate concerns, beginning with removal of Haysem's body from the scene. Then within 15 minutes it was confirmed that there was one more missing student – Mohamed Fofana.

It was believed he was likely in close proximity to where Haysem Sani had been found. Saint Paul emergency responders knew little else, including how long it would take to find and remove Mohamed. But due to the large amount of sand and rock that had fallen from the bluff sides little else was clear except that this was now a "recovery" rather than a life-saving situation.

Just several hundred yards away, up on the Cherokee Park bluff line, Mohamed's parents, family and other Guinean friends were now waiting helplessly. Like other parents of Peter Hobart students on the field trip they had received phone calls from the school that there had been an accident but few other details.

"I got a call at my workplace and I said, 'Where is this Lilydale Park? I had never been there before," remembered Lancine. "I quick called Madosu and went home to pick her up."

Almost simultaneously, a relative called to tell her to turn on her TV to see first news reports on the landslide. No names were then known. But it was mentioned that at least one child remained missing. Madosu immediately threw on her coat and went outside and began walking in the direction that Lancine would be coming to pick her up.

"I could not stand it. I just kept thinking about how he (Mohamed) was out there somewhere and he could be cold and scared," she said of her first born child. "All kinds of things were going through my head. I had to get there."

The Fofanas did not make it to the scene until well after 3pm, after experiencing their own frustrating detours and delays navigating Lilydale Park's expansive geography. They finally made their way to the Cherokee Park bluff where other supportive members of the Guinean community would also soon begin arriving. Included was Imam Mohammed Dukaly from their Brooklyn Center mosque, who would become the family's informal spokesperson through most of the ordeal to follow.

The bluff area was barricaded off and crowded with police and fire department vehicles from multiple jurisdictions, media with cameras, neighborhood residents and onlookers. The Fofana family and friends were shepherded aside to begin hours of helpless waiting. Occasional updates from city officials offered little information except to confirm that their son, Mohamed, was still missing.

By this time other equally anxious Peter Hobart parents had all, per telephone instructions, gone directly to the school. They knew almost nothing else other than what had been broadcast through the media about the Lilydale Park catastrophe.

In late afternoon, field trip buses returned to the St. Louis Park school. Understandably shaken students were quickly taken inside, past gathered media. There they were tearfully reunited with their parents – exceptions being the Sani and the Fofana families, as well as Devin Meldahl and his mother who were at the hospital.

Meanwhile, Saint Paul rescue teams continued trying to find the best and safest ways to remove debris from the location where they believed Mohamed was buried. The field trip group photo taken earlier provided some clues. Yet it remained something of a Blind Man's Bluff effort.

The Fire Department first lowered hoses from the top of the bluff and began several hours of "hydraulic excavation" to wash away dirt and rocks. Then it was decided that police cadaver dogs should be utilized, though Lancine and Madosu were not told - partly out of sensitivity to their Muslim faith's mixed feelings about canines. The police dogs fairly soon made "hits" in the middle of a debris pile about eight feet from the collapsed wall. They began to feel confident of the location of Mohamed's body.

However, by now it was well past sunset and more water was flowing down the bluff into the area. Fire Marshall Steve Zaccard would send an email at 9:03pm to top city officials, including Mayor Coleman.

"The rain has started up again making the flowing water causing further erosion is a problem again," he wrote, his hurried grammatical errors still leaving little doubt about the situation.

Two Minnesota Department of Natural Resources geologists and another from the Minnesota Geological Service had been called in to help assess risks to emergency personnel from falling rocks and the general instability of the bluff. At their advice, a large overhanging tree was removed before it might topple onto rescue crews.

But the darkened ravine was becoming increasingly dangerous for emergency workers. At 9:30 pm it was decided to discontinue efforts until the following morning's light.

For the Fofanas it was, of course, heartbreaking news. But they accepted it with what would come to be recognized as their usual grace, not complaining about the decision. City officials were impressed by their expressions of appreciation for the emergency workers' efforts and concern for their safety. Yet they obviously always had their son in the forefront of their thoughts.

"I had never thought that Mohamed had passed. It never occurred to me. But when they told us they still hadn't found him, I knew," said Lancine, who recognized that a dividing line had now been crossed. He intuitively knew that the rescue mission had become a recovery mission.

"All I could think about was him being out there alone in the dark by himself," said Madosu, admitting to having been unsure what to think at the time. "I just knew I didn't want to leave but we had to."

They returned to their Brooklyn Park home where the parents would have to try to explain the situation to their remaining twin sons and other family members. After a sleepless night, the Fofanas would return at break of dawn the next morning.

Mayor Chris Coleman was there to greet them, offering condolences and promises to double the number of rescue workers looking for their son. Not mentioned was Asst. Fire Chief Smith's assessment the day before that there were already too many personnel at the site, potentially inhibiting rescue efforts and creating more safety risks.

Regardless, rescue teams renewed the search at approximately 9:30 am on May 23. This time it did not take much digging before Mohamed's shirt was spotted underneath rubble, near the spot indicated by the canine patrol the previous evening.

After about another hour's worth of digging and hydraulic excavation, Mohamed's corpse was removed from the Lilydale earth. He had suffered multiple traumatic injuries from debris hitting him during the collapse, according to official reports – likely a quick death. After being brought to the top of the Lilydale Park bluff, he was able to be viewed, in part, by his grieving parents and other family members. They briefly held his hand before he was taken to the medical examiner's facilities.

Mohamed's school backpack, containing papers and a diary, was found under rubble at the accident scene.

Rescue team members in Cherokee Park, including Minnesota DNR geologist Dr. Carrie Jennings, were deeply impacted by witnessing the Fofana family's handling of the almost unimaginable situation.

"It broke my heart because they were such beautiful people. They looked royal," remembered Dr. Jennings of Lancine and Madosu. "And when the women wailed it was an expression of grief you don't get in this culture. They made this sound that was almost unworldly."

"They cried out in unison. I'll never forget that. My heart went out to that family," agreed fellow DNR geologist Heather Arends.

"When we brought him up to the top it was unbelievable to see the grief and anguish they were going through, but also the dignity," seconded Rick Larkin, then director of Saint Paul Emergency Management Services, speaking of Mohamed's parents. "They were still thanking all the firefighters and everyone who had helped with the search. It was incredibly touching to hear that, all the while they have suffered so much."

Lancine has continued to praise all the first responders at Lilydale Park among his first recollections of those two fateful days

"Those people were going to do their best, they were so good. They really, really cared, like they were looking for their own son, I had no doubt," he said, pausing in the midst of describing his mix of emotions. "But I never thought I would see Mohamed dead. To be honest, it was hard to accept that Mohamed was gone and I was in shock."

His mother was perhaps even more in disbelief.

"It was so hard to believe. I still kept hoping he was out there somewhere, maybe with a broken ankle or something, and that they would find him," said Madosu of the shock. She barely remembers kissing her dead son before having to be helped to their vehicle. "I didn't know how to feel after I saw him."

But the Fofanas would soon regain their footing. With other family obligations including two younger sons, the couple knew they had to remain strong.

Twins Hassan and Al-Seny were in their first year of school at Peter Hobart Elementary. Then of course there were funeral and memorial services, both Islamic and secular, to be planned in short order. Members of the Fofana family in West Africa also had to be notified to begin planning their own memorial services. The next several weeks were a blur, both Lancine and Madosu recalled.

Family and many Twin Cities Guinean community members flocked to the Fofanas' North Minneapolis home, bringing sympathy nearly round-the-clock. In the midst of their pain, Lancine and Madosu received loving attention but also had a host of responsibilities to preoccupy them. Photos of Mohamed were put on display, many of which were subsequently taken as mementos by friends.

"We had people at our house for like two weeks," recalled Madosu. "They were there to console us and bring food. Or if we ran out of food to go get some. We all just shared everything. That is the way we are."

On the family refrigerator was a homemade Mother's Day card. It read "Dear Mom, you are a wonderful cook. I love it when you make chicken with noodles. You are helpful. Thanks for cleaning and washing my clothes. You're funny and tell great jokes."

The card was signed, "Mohamed Fofana." His mother

would understandably want to leave it there for weeks.

"Those days were really a cloud for us both. With all the people there to console us you didn't feel as much," remembered Lancine. "Once the people would leave or when you were alone, then you would feel the pain. Every second you think about your son. Every second you feel."

Yet neither parent recalls feeling totally overcome with their grief, partly because of the support network from family and friends and partly because their Muslim faith and other beliefs helped them withstand the pain. Just as sadness was in the air, there was also a certain kind of stoicism.

Culture and history may provide further explanation. Theirs was a traditional response to an all-too-familiar type of tragedy in Guinean life, suggest those with familiarity. Especially for those coming from gold-mining areas, Mohamed's death may have had a certain quality of deja vu.

"It's a culture that has been influenced for years, centuries, by how fragile life is – especially for children," explained Kurt Swanson, a long-time Fofana family friend who lived in Guinea for over 10 years as a mission worker. "Fatalism is both part of Islamic teaching and is a kind of a coping mechanism, which doesn't at all mean they don't care. It's maybe a way to ease the pain."

The gathering of family and Guinean community members certainly did help provide something of a cocoon in the midst of, not only normal grief, but also the glare of media attention. TV trucks parked outside and sometimes photographers and reporters came inside to talk with the always accommodating Fofana family.

"In the aftermath of the tragedy, I've seen very few people with as much grace. They were so approving of everyone and didn't carry anger," concluded Swanson. "I can't say enough good about the family."

Stories about the death of Mohamed and Haysem Sani were broadcast not only nationwide but also internationally.

I happened to be with a medical mission group in Nicaragua when I first heard of the accident via social media. I was then able to read about some circumstances of the landslide online and even talked with a Saint Paul newspaper reporter inquiring about Friends of Lilydale's perspective.

Most media accounts were focused on the universally understandable story of tragedy interrupting a school field trip. But they also often wove in another curious narrative that contained a different, more Western type of fatalism. In that telling, the children's deaths were almost predetermined by non-human forces.

Some media and public comments suggested fickle, or even cruel, Mother Nature had struck suddenly without reason. Her life-giving rains were in this scenario seen as life-taking. Searching for further explanation for the landslide became almost a pointless exercise under this logic.

By extension, it seemed that unrefined Lilydale Park practically became a villain in some media accounts. It was described as a place whose untamed nature - rather than its known human alterations such as historic bluff excavations and ongoing storm-water erosion - created unpredictable danger.

This story line fit well with a City of Saint Paul's narrative that developed very quickly to explain the "unimaginable and unprecedented tragedy." Mayor's Office Communications Director Joe Campbell quickly wrote up a list of talking points about the landslide in Lilydale Park. He coordinated city staff messaging throughout all departments from the earliest days.

"This was unprecedented. What happened there was a major land mass movement that no one could have predicted," said Parks & Recreation spokesperson Brad Meyer, ignoring both the 2009 consultant study and the huge 2011 landslide just 75 yards away from where Mohamed and Haysem died.

"There is no indication prior to this happening that this sort of thing could have occurred," seconded Mike Hahm, Director of Saint Paul Parks and Recreation, also staying on message at a press conference the day after the two boys' deaths.

Mayor Coleman followed Hah to the mic. He described

his sorrow over the events and sympathy for the families of the deceased St. Louis Park students.

"It was a tragic day in the City of Saint Paul, one that began filled with hope and excitement for these children and that has forever altered the many families in our community," said Coleman.

He defended the city's fossil permitting regardless of weather conditions by noting that he lived just a few blocks from Lilydale Park. "I have gone in the rain. I have gone in the sun. I have gone in the snow," he said.

But the Saint Paul Mayor was also quick to argue that the permit's standard language requiring fossil-hunters to sign a liability waiver was clear and sufficient warning of all hazards. "These are natural areas. ...There are dangers anytime you are in a natural area like this. ...This wasn't because of any particular threat or concern."

Coleman announced that the fossil grounds would be closed for the indefinite future while causes of the landslide were fully studied, just in case there were ongoing safety concerns. He specifically noted that he had asked for help from State of Minnesota DNR geologists. That presumably referred to Dr. Jennings and others who had been invited to help the day Mohamed and Haysem Sani died.

It was all fairly boilerplate PR responses by the Mayor that arguably reflected understandable caution by city officials operating with still limited information in the first few days after the May 22, 2013 disaster.

But then Coleman responded oddly to a question about the possible construction impacts in the area of the accident. Road graders and other equipment could still be seen scattered about Cherokee Park bluff directly above Lilydale Park as a road and trail project was being completed.

"There was no indication at all that any of the activity that was done in the park really was connected to this incident," Coleman said.

Yet he then continued by making curious reference to a different project about which no one had asked, and likely no reporter had knowledge. Less visible in Cherokee Park was reconstruction of a storm-water culvert that had been completed just a few days before. It channeled large amounts of water underneath the new road and trail and into Lilydale Park

"There was some work on a drainage system, but that was not directly impacting this area at all," said Coleman in his unsolicited denial.

It was an answer that drew little or no attention at the time. Reporters either had no understanding nor any curiosity about the Mayor's brief reference to the city's unplugging of the nearby 60-inch round storm-water culvert. The project increased the amount of water going directly into the ravine and canyon where the tragedy happened.

Undoubtedly neither engineers nor Coleman had anticipated all impacts. Yet Mother Nature certainly had nothing to do with making that decision nor with efforts to deny and cover up human roles in the tragedy.

Before and after:
To the right, Peter Hobart
Elementary students, teachers
and chaperones look for
fossils in Lilydale Park just
minutes before an undercut
ravine wall (left center) would
collapse on them. Note the
waterfall (upper right) fed by
the Cherokee Park stormwater
culvert which had already
helped push corrugated metal
and other debris into the
ravine below.
Credit Shane Boettcher

Saint Paul firefighters,
police and other
emergency responders
(left) struggle to find
children buried under
rock and sand from the
landslide. Note the lack
of digging tools
available to help their
heroic efforts, as well as
the collapsed ravine
ledge on the upper left.
Credit: City of Saint Paul

Lancine and Madosu waited over five years to see the landslide site of their son Mohamed's death on May 22, 2013.

While first responders raced by to Cherokee Park bluff, teachers tried to explain to 911 operators that they were waiting at a locked gate on Hwy. 13 which provided best access to the accident site.

Chapter 4

"Anything that's human is mentionable, and anything that is mentionable can be more manageable. When we can talk about our feelings, they become less overwhelming, less upsetting, and less scary. "
—**Fred Rogers**

S hock waves from the May 22, 2013 tragic events in Lilydale Park continued to ripple daily for weeks. Most happened quietly or behind closed doors. Usually it was school children, family members, first responders or other powerless victims trying to cope with the impacts of an experience beyond their control. Sometimes it was the powerful trying to spin understanding of an experience over which they wanted to keep control.

Parents who picked up stunned fourth graders at Peter Hobart Elementary that afternoon must have wished they were empowered to turn back time. Many had dropped off or watched their children get on buses in the morning while carrying joyful anticipation on their faces. Now their sons and daughters' eyes were full of tears and horror after seeing their classmates seriously injured or killed. Trying to help nine and ten-year-olds comprehend the meaning of tragedy and death was suddenly the consuming task of everyone. It wasn't one that would end soon.

"I remember that day like it was perpetually yesterday. I've never been so scared in my life," said Andraya Lund, recounting the phone call that she and other parents received notifying them only that there had been an accident on the Lilydale Park field trip. She and other parents were told to come immediately to Peter Hobart School.

Lund was friends with chaperones on the trip and was quickly able to find out her daughter was safe. But she also learned that there were two missing, unidentified, students.

Principal Shelley Nielsen directly contacted the parents of Mohamed, Haysem and Devon to tell them everything that was known about their children. But District officials felt they had to be tight-mouthed with others while the search continued. Most parents thus had few details about what had happened on the field trip other than through sketchy, sometimes inaccurate media reports. They often had no way of knowing whether their own children had been injured until the buses arrived back at the school around 4 pm.

Anne Schultz had already learned of the Lilydale Park tragedy from television news briefs. She had the advantage of knowing her daughter was safe thanks to a text from a chaperone friend on the field trip. She even learned that it was four boys who had been physically hurt or missing. But that partial news, and other information that filtered out, didn't entirely ease any parent's concerns as they waited for the buses to return from Lilydale Park.

"You could just see the panic of other parents who had

boys," she remembered. "Everybody was just holding their breath. ...They (the school district) wasn't telling us much because I don't think they knew much."

The chaos of the first hours after the accident had every public agency scrambling to know how to respond to the unusual circumstances. School officials were as dependent as anyone on what information it could receive from Saint Paul and emergency response officials.

"In a crisis of this nature there were so many jurisdictions involved. ... It became a real challenge just to follow along with the players," agreed St. Louis Park District communications director Sara Thompson, describing dozens of phone calls in the immediate hours after the landslide to other government and emergency agencies as well as to all of the impacted families.

"I completely understand the criticism. But we worked very hard with the information we had. We always feel like it's important not to make a guess," she added.

But the lack of complete information about the Lilydale Park tragedy obviously was most stressful for parents of children on the field trip. Some also had other children at Peter Hobart Elementary, who had been released from classes and had to be picked up and cared for, along with waiting for the returning fourth graders.

"Parents were all there in the cafeteria looking out the window for the bus. You could feel the panic in that room," Lund said. "Then to see the look of fear on those kids' faces. ..."

Adding to the stress were the media, camera trucks and lights already camped outside Peter Hobart when the field trip buses returned to Peter Hobart Elementary. They were looking for reactions to the still-unfolding tragedy in Lilydale Park and arguably just doing their jobs as journalists in seeking more information on behalf of the general public. But it set up a clash in values with St. Louis Park parents who during that time period in particular saw protection of student and family privacy as their top priorities.

Attempts to create a buffer only partly succeeded. Thompson noted that she arranged to have fire trucks in front of the school building to block of media vehicles. Teachers and chaperones formed a human shield to further protect the children getting off the buses from TV cameras and reporters' questions.

It would succeed initially, but some media would wait for hours outside the school. Others returned in following days with some parents reporting that children on foot would be followed down the street by reporters. Their efforts to capture reactions and get comments from parents and children leaving Peter Hobart would be seen as intrusive by many and began a too-often adversarial relationship.

"It felt very violating sometimes," said parent Derek Burrows Reise. "It became a big challenge to know how to deal with the media doing their job, while still protecting the kids and the community."

District officials were especially guarded in comments that first day. Superintendent Debra Bowers made only an online statement to media.

"This is an incredibly sad time for our schools and our entire school community," she said. "We, like everyone, want to understand how this tragedy occurred. But today we ask for your continued thoughts and prayers for everyone involved."

School officials would soon be criticized in the media for allowing the field trip to Lilydale, especially after several days of heavy rains previous to the field trip. Implied was the idea that teachers should have realized the danger posed by saturation of the park's bluff areas.

Surprisingly few parents of Peter Hobart students would share in that criticism. Most praised teachers and administrators for how well they responded to the tragedy, especially in the early days.

St. Louis Park Schools also gained kudos for their support of victims. They immediately lined up grief counselors, therapy dogs and other psychological services to students, parents and staff. All would need to be in place quickly – and some for a considerable period of time – as Peter Hobart classes would resume as usual the next day.

But the makeshift memorial that quickly went up outside the school made clear that things were not normal. Balloons, teddy bears, poems and bouquets of flowers dedicated to Mohamed and Haysem were placed there by community members and others wanting to show their sympathy. A similar, but smaller, display would soon be put up outside the bluff top entrance to Lilydale Park in Cherokee Park. The young fossil-hunters' horrific accident affected many people throughout the Twin Cities area and well beyond.

"I couldn't imagine sending them off to school for a field trip and not seeing them again. My heart just goes out to the parents," said Richfield resident Brittany

Frechette, telling local SunSailor reporter Seth Rowe that she decided to visit the school after hearing about the tragedy on the news.

"It's just awful," St. Louis Park parent Jennifer Vought added, as she placed down flowers and a note. "There's just no words to explain the pain, that the family's feeling. I just feel very sad."

Sympathetic notes came individuals and from groups. St. Louis Park High School students, who had recently lost two classmates to unrelated sudden accidental deaths, started a campaign to sign large cards and make paper flowers for Peter Hobart Elementary students. Supportive phone calls came into the school from all around the metro area. Local businesses and individuals would soon come forward to offer help and money to the impacted families. Saint Paul police, fire and other emergency responders made meaningful appearances at memorials and other events.

"The outpouring of support was amazing," said Thompson. "On any given day, 20 members of the community were showing up, giving items, offering to help any way they could. It was nothing short of a miracle in a really dark time."

Political figures were also quick to jump into action with statements of regret, and concern. Included were two U.S. Senators, several members of Congress and multiple local officials – obviously including the mayors of Saint Paul and St. Louis Park. Most could be described as fairly predictable, without suggesting insincerity. They also reflected the widespread public reaction to the Lilydale Park tragedy.

Perhaps most noteworthy was the dramatic appearance of Minnesota Governor Mark Dayton at Peter Hobart Elementary on May 24.

Students and staff were assembled outside, seated near the playground and soccer fields that classmates Mohamed and Haysem had both loved. Everyone expected to hear standard words of condolence. To the surprise of all, they heard Dayton tell how he had lost one of his own best friends in a rock slide some years before. He went on to describe his emotions at learning the news.

"I remember the horror I felt, the shock and the disbelief," said the Governor. "I said why? Why did not just a bad thing happen to a good person, but why did a terrible thing happen to a terrific person?

"I can't give you an answer for why? We live in a very safe place here, probably the safest the world has ever been since humans started to be here," said Dayton, making a comparison to the prehistoric world – perhaps to connect with the young fossil-hunters around him. "Minnesota is probably one of the safest places in the world and St. Louis Park is probably one of the safest places in Minnesota. And yet, a terrible thing like this can happen.

"I wish I could say something to make you feel better. I wish I can say something to explain why this terrible thing happened. I can't. But I know looking and seeing all of you, Haysem and Mohamed's spirit will be carried on through all of you," concluded the Governor.

The speech topped local evening TV news broadcasts and was carried in newspapers across the country. At least for the first few days after the Lilydale Park tragedy, media generally focused on community solidarity and positive expressions of sympathy and concern for the victims families and surviving classmates. Dayton's address was a feel good moment in the midst of a time of darkness for everyone connected to what happened in Lilydale Park.

The Governor's speech got some mixed, but mostly positive, reactions in the Peter Hobart community.

"That was a PR thing. It wasn't for the kids. Most of them didn't know who he was," concluded Lund. "But it was probably good for the parents and administrators."

Thompson insisted that the event sprang entirely from Dayton's heart-felt personal interest in speaking to the children.

"Never in the middle of a crisis have I had a Governor schedule a visit to a school," she said, noting her own surprise. "But it really was a great show of strength, solidarity and perseverance."

"I think most people appreciated the Governor coming," agreed Reise. "It was a little bit awkward sometimes just because he's Mark Dayton. But I think he was very sincere and it was a nice gesture."

******

Feel good moments would be few however in immediate days after the May 22, 2013 tragedy.

Doubts about responsibility for the Lilydale Park field trip debacle were planted early on by some Saint Paul officials, pointing to a waiver clause in the fossil hunting permit signed by a Peter Hobart teacher. Its boilerplate, generic language was argued to be an all-purpose protection to the city.

"The park user fully acknowledges that some of the conditions and locations within the Lilydale Regional Park area are hazardous to persons or property and park user specifically assumes the liability of the City of St. Paul as such claims or injuries may arise to persons and property due to its unsafe conditions," read the permit, in part.

Questions of responsibility further rose to the surface at a sometimes heated May 23 press conference. St. Louis Park School District officials were clearly put on the run after being asked about why the field trip hadn't been canceled after heavy rains in previous days. Saint Paul's liability waiver was also brought up.

The event began with Peter Hobart principal Shelley Nielsen describing positive conversations with the Fofana and Sani families, though still refusing to use their already widely-known names. Media were clearly irritated at what they perceived as a lack of openness. But Nielsen tried to ask for patience while noting the school's main focus was on dealing with the impacts of the landslide deaths for all the fourth graders.

"For many of our students, this is maybe the very first time they've dealt with a tragedy of this magnitude, losing a classmate or losing anyone at all in this life," she said. "We're blessed in the community to have a tremendous amount of support."

However things went south when media asked about weather conditions and whether parents had been notified about potential hazards in the Lilydale Park field trip. Other reporters pressed for more information on victims and teachers names and other information that District officials felt they could not legally divulge at that time.

Thompson then announced that officials would not answer any more questions, ending the press conference with reporters shouting questions that went unanswered. It was the beginning of a frequently contentious relationship with media, that sometimes left the school district looking increasingly defensive and non-transparent.

"We work very hard in St. Louis Park to be very responsive to our stakeholders and our public," the district's communications director said later in describing the decision to end the press conference. "But the questions had taken a turn toward personal staff and student data. ... It's a delicate dance sometimes and we all do our best to find a place in the middle serving the public good."

By contrast, Saint Paul officials did a different dance. They followed advice from the top, notably Mayor Chris Coleman, and found more success in turning (very occasionally) tough media questions toward more favorable directions.

City marketing director Jake Spano, who then also happened to be a St. Louis Park city council member and is now currently that city's mayor, explained the strategy in a critique of the ill-fated school district press conference.

"Our city comm team was there and warned them that these questions would come up and that they should answer honestly, and then pivot as CBC (Coleman's initials) mentioned yesterday. Too bad the school district didn't take our advice," wrote Spano in an email to a few key Saint Paul city leaders.

Thompson does not recall any conversations with Spano, at the time, about the Lilydale Park tragedy, or communications strategy.

"It was very tragic and sad and very personal from our side with all of the St. Louis Park students and families involved," she concluded of the aborted press conference. "But it also scaled very quickly to being political. ... So that creates a lot of challenges in terms of messaging."

Messaging from the Saint Paul side clearly wasn't designed to help school officials. They were left to fend off tough questions about their decision to go ahead with the field trip in rainy conditions and particularly the adequacy of their student permitting process.

Blaming-the-victim thinking was arguably aided by the imposed silence, immediately after the accident, that city officials put on first responders. Included was Assistant Saint Paul Fire Chief Matt Simpson., a veteran Lilydale Park fossil-hunter himself.

"That's a place I visited with both of my sons. It didn't represent itself as dangerous by any means," he would be able to say years later. "Those teachers wouldn't have knowingly put those kids in that danger. We all have to be fair to that."

But such public messages were extremely rare in City Hall during the crucial early days after the tragedy.

Saint Paul Parks and Recreation officials instead chose

to repeatedly note how St. Louis Park District did not take the same legally protective measures as some fossil-hunting groups. A number of the well-over-400 school groups receiving fossil permits annually would send to parents special information about potential risks in Lilydale Park, the city said. Whether intended or not, that claim served to at least temporarily pivot discussion from the legality of the city's own vaguely-worded waiver statement.

It was a debate that would continue for months to come, with neither governmental body ultimately coming out looking good. But in early public perceptions, St. Louis Park school officials and Peter Hobart staff were most clearly put on the defensive.

Those staff who had been on the Lilydale Park field trip had, of course, their own emotional issues to focus on - even as they needed to remain strong in front of at-least-equally troubled students. It no doubt added to communication walls that for some remain difficult to scale to this day.

City employees, especially first responders, certainly also had their own difficulties stemming from the trauma of the landslide deaths. A number reportedly needed and sought personal counseling after seeing their heroic efforts fail. Even among those with experience in such situations, it was an especially scarring event. Emails among staff from all departments indicated sincere shock and distress at witnessing, or even hearing of, the deaths of two children in a Saint Paul park.

Special group meetings with counselors were set up for the approximately 52 firefighters who responded to the

Lilydale Park landslide calls.

"This incident brought out the parent, grandparent, aunt, uncle, brother and sister in all of us," wrote Saint Paul firefighter David Mathison in an email. "We need to take time to reflect on what we saw, what we did, and to make sure our co-workers and ourselves are able to reach out to one another."

But top Saint Paul City Hall leaders never relaxed their communications priorities, even late into the night of May 22, 2013. As emergency crews were still desperately trying to figure out how to deal with flowing water and dangerous, eroding bluffs that blocked progress in finding Mohamed's body, Mayor's office PR guru Joe Campbell was sending an email to Fire Marshall Steve Zaccard. He was told to be sure to have a 7 am update ready for him.

All questions from media were already being referred to Campbell or Parks' spokesperson Brad Meyer. Within days City Hall put a ban on all interviews with first responders and emergency personnel involved in the Lilydale Park catastrophe. Even normal, seemingly non-threatening human interest media requests were denied.

Campbell would also soon send out notice that he must personally review all Minnesota Data Practices Act requests to any city department before any public information was released. It was just one of several interesting interpretations of freedom of information statutes that was encountered in the process of doing my own journalistic requests to the City of Saint Paul.

The city's concerns about media and public scrutiny were quickly shown to be warranted. By the morning of May 23, Campbell had received a query from a local TV producer about a city website link to a document suggesting that Lilydale bluff erosion and related safety concerns had been known since 2012. The Environmental Assessment Worksheet referred to had been done at the request of Friends of Lilydale Park and noted that bluff erosion concerns had been pointed out to the city since at least 2009.

But the TV piece never ran. Campbell, with the help of city environmental projects director Anne Hunt, apparently fended off that half-hearted attempt to look critically at warning signs before the 2013 tragedy.

However the heat was potentially growing, with more questions arising about evidence of earlier landslides in both Lilydale Park and nearby areas. Articles mentioned that just a couple years before boulders had come crashing down into a West Side neighborhood bakery. My wife, Grit Youngquist, told a *St. Paul Pioneer Press* reporter about the fore-mentioned 2011 North Knob mudslide in Lilydale Park. - though again the information was never seriously followed investigated.

Somehow Mike Hahm, Director of Saint Paul Parks and Recreation, got away simply by responding that he was unaware of the incident. This came despite emails and other documented evidence showing at least a half dozen high level department employees had clear knowledge of the previous landslide.

It was a close call that perhaps helped trigger a new approach by Saint Paul leaders determined not to be put on the defensive. They would again pivot, and gain time.

On the morning of March 24, the city put out a press release announcing the hiring of a civil engineering firm to examine the collapse site in Lilydale Park in order to determine its cause. Soil drillings and other tests would begin within days, providing a positive image of action on the issue.

Saint Paul officials would reap other benefits. Included would be an ability to remain silent until an unspecified future date when investigation of the May 22, 2013 landslide was completed by the engineering firm.

"With particular expertise in the evaluation of collapses and natural disasters, we expect their work to provide us with a better comprehension of what caused this tragic accident," said Hahm in the press release.

He was referring to a Fargo-based engineering firm, Northern Technologies Incorporated, that had been founded in 1997, about the time of that state's oil and fracking boom. They were known for their soil-boring, well contracting and construction material testing services and were looking to build their business in the Twin Cities area. No record can be found of NTI's previous experience in major investigations such as the Lilydale Park landslide.

Hahm's reference to NTI's expertise in natural disasters was unevidenced. Equally curiously, a city email uncovered later indicated that the firm was actually hired by the city's Public Works department not by the Parks director. Why that department, whose only connection to Lilydale Park was the storm sewers emptying water from Cherokee bluff, would choose the firm to head the investigation of the "natural" catastrophe was also unexplained.

Regardless, it was certainly true that NTI had direct experience in collapses.

Almost exactly one year before their announced hiring by the City of Saint Paul they had been sued, along with two other contractors involved in the collapse of the North Dakota State University's main academic building. Fortunately no one had been hurt in an overnight near buckling-in-half of the recently-expanded structure. The university lawsuit claimed it was caused by engineering negligence and poor soil testing.

NTI would respond by calling the ground collapse under the university building "a mere accident and an Act of God."

The lawsuit was eventually settled out-of-court with NDSU receiving over $3 million from NTI and the other contractors.

Chapter 5

Who trusted God was love indeed
And love Creation's final law
Tho' Nature, red in tooth and claw
With ravine, shriek'd against his creed

-Lord Alfred Tennyson

Saint Paul residents and others familiar with Lilydale Park were as stunned and heartbroken as anyone in the days immediately following the May 22, 2013 tragedy. Nearly everyone remembers where they were when they first heard the horrible news.

Neighbors created their own small memorial at the bluff entrance to the Brickyard Trail where the bodies had been brought up from the ravine below. Expressions of sympathy for children, and their families, caught in the landslide dominated local newspapers and social media for days. The event likely caused many to consider the relationship between choices and fate in everyone's life.

Many social media commentators noted that locals had long known how dangerous the bluffs could be after a period of rain. A few remarked how it could easily have been neighborhood children instead of children from out-of-town on a field trip who had been buried under rock and sand. A few echoed the official city line that Peter Hobart field trip leaders should have realized the risk they were taking. But sympathy for the students and families was more common - mixed with questions about the future of the bluff area which was beloved for its fossil-hunting, dog-walking, hiking, bird and wildlife-watching and other activities.

For Friends of Lilydale Park, the entire bluff area's closing to the public created a different kind of tragedy – albeit one that certainly paled in comparison to the loss of human life. Combined with areas of the park that had been closed for the city's ambitious road and trail construction projects in the Mississippi floodplain, this meant that virtually the entire park would be shut down for the summer and into the foreseeable future. This included the popular Vento's View lookout, and even trails and fossil areas that were far from any danger. The city's over-reaction, likely based more on self-protective legal concerns than true safety concerns, would be additional punishment for those who had warned of the park's need for TLC.

My personal shock at the events in Lilydale Park came in two major waves, the first on hearing about the deaths. The second wave came a few days later upon return from a trip to Nicaragua, a country that has known more than its share of both natural and human-made disasters.

Visiting the landslide site, just a few blocks from my West Side neighborhood home, I had no trouble finding the spot roughly described in newspaper articles. Yellow police tape wrapped around trees all over the bluff top made the location all the more obvious. The scene was surreal in its serenity that day. But it was easy to look down the hill past uprooted trees to see the tons of rock and sand that had come crashing down. One did not want to contemplate how the two children were buried as well as the shattered psyches of so many other young people and adults.

However, my greatest shock came when I climbed back up from the ravine and crossed the newly repaved and expanded Cherokee Boulevard roadway and parallel trail. There, in a Cherokee Park gully less than 50 yards to the east, were clear signs of yet another major construction project. My shock came because I had no idea this work was going to happen, despite having recently been a neighborhood representative on the city's design task force that had planned the road and trail project on the bluff above Lilydale Park.

Of course, by this time FOL's place in the decision-making process had been made clear. Lead Parks planner Alice Messer had taken me aside to politely, but firmly, make clear that there would be no major changes considered to "her" Cherokee Boulevard project. At that time we were also engaged in (ultimately fruitless) negotiations with Parks on their Lilydale Park Master Plan designs. So I had remained largely un-challenging about what had seemed a relatively innocuous plan for road and bike trail improvements in that area.

To my everlasting regret, I did not join another neighborhood member who had wanted to close Cherokee Boulevard to vehicles going through the park. His focus was on traffic.

But a road closure may have helped stop the chain of events leading to the tragedy of May 22, 2013. For it was to protect their new roadway asphalt from a problem with standing water during rains, that city staff decided to give bluff-top storm-water a boost in making its way downhill into the very Lilydale Park ravine leading to where the children were killed.

Parks staff, in conjunction with Public Works, had chosen to redesign and freshly excavate the area leading to an aged storm-water culvert running under the roadway and trail. Shrubs and other growth were removed, with new rip-rap lining the bottom, to discourage saturation into the soil. It was an effort to fix "plugged catch basins" that were slowing the flow of storm-water from both Cherokee Boulevard and an adjoining 36-acres, including West St. Paul and Mendota Heights neighborhoods. These drainage changes added to the volume of water going through the remodeled culvert.

For some reason, the issue had never been brought up in public planning sessions before the project construction got underway. But even to my novice engineering eye it appeared a major alteration that must have impacted the amount and speed of storm-water flowing through the culvert into the Lilydale Park accident site.

There was no work crew there that weekend day to ask about the Cherokee Park gully and culvert project. But nearby I saw other city workers planting trees alongside the new trail - though the plantings would never come near the number or size of the old growth arbor that Parks had taken out for their trail and road work.

I bicycled up to an older man wearing a t-shirt bearing a CCC logo who appeared to be supervising several younger workers. We quickly struck up a conversation about the Civilian Conservation Corps, a New Deal-era program employing young men in the 1930s on a variety of environmental, construction and other public service projects that helped shape Minnesota's relationship with natural resources. I learned his father had been a lumberjack at a northwoods CCC operation.

We then shifted back to his volunteer work there at the edge of Lilydale Park - and the recent tragedy.

"My son does a lot of ice climbing in that area and tried to warn his superiors at Parks that the area was in trouble," he said, with a shrug. "They didn't listen and now this whole bluff area is closed down. Who knows if it will ever get straightened out? It's just a shame."

Only later was I able to determine his son's identity. At the time I didn't fully understand the significance of his account, nor did I think to ask his name. But I already knew there were plenty of questions to be answered. There had been a lot more going on in Lilydale Park than an unpredictable act of God or Mother Nature.

In fairness, some Saint Paul officials were immediately trying to establish what had happened those fateful days. On May 23, 2013 immediately after Mohamed's body was found and rescue workers efforts were terminated, Emergency Response director Rick Larkin sent out a memo to all agencies declaring that a standard After Action Review (AAR) should soon be held. Better understanding and communication of geographic locations in Lilydale Park was immediately identified as a top need.

But discussion of the AAR process soon appeared to vanish, except among communication specialists like Campbell, Meyer and Fire Department PR coordinator, Howie Padilla. The priority clearly was not on sharing and learning from experience while memories of the disaster were fresh. Instead, most city communications appeared focused on getting correct names of all involved in the Lilydale Park incident. The importance of that was to ensure that they would receive a personal thank you note from Mayor Coleman.

Other priorities discussed in emails following the landslide included the wording on signs to be posted around Lilydale Park. Original suggestions included the warning: "Do not proceed past this point – unstable conditions."

But after being run past the City Attorney's office, it was decided that such wording might indicate the city had been aware of a dangerous condition for some time. The final solution was a more innocuous "Do not proceed beyond this point: rock slides have recently occurred."

Legal liability and public relations concerns were clearly gaining the upper hand in Saint Paul decision-making. As time went on, the slippery slope from open and honest discussion of the Lilydale Park incident grew even more treacherous.

*****

The Peter Hobart Elementary School community meanwhile had its own difficult climb after the events of May 22, 2013.

Top priority was understandably helping children try to make sense of having classmates either killed or injured before their eyes. Parents and educators, who themselves did not have a totally clear understanding of what happened that day, had to help young students understand a world in which a fun fossil hunt in a park suddenly turned into an encounter with death.

"Kids were shell-shocked. ... It's really hard for kids that age to process grief like that. You think that death only happens to old people," observed parent and PTO president Andraya Lund. "The parents were just as confused."

Peter Hobart Elementary, the day after the catastrophe and the remaining month of the school year, was anything but normal. District officials initially allowed teachers and staff extra resources and complete flexibility to respond in any way that seemed appropriate. Parents, along with their children, were invited to attend special sessions that focused on emotional needs as much as scholastic exercises.

"They all got in a circle and we went around and everyone had a chance to talk about Mohamed and Haysem and how they were feeling," parent Stacy Atlas recalled. "There were a lot of tears and questions that were hard to answer. But Sarah (Reichart) was so amazing and calm the kids really responded to her lead. By the time they went to gym and started playing together things were already a little better – at least for awhile."

Schultz attended school with her daughter, Grace, for most of the remaining two weeks in the school year. She saw a contrast in how the two fourth grade classes handled processing the tragic event. In contrast to Reichart's classes which continued open discussion, Penny Dupris' class returned to more normal lessons after the first day.

"I think they were told not to do that any more. I think she was getting a lot of direction from the school (district) and the lawyers," said Schultz, referring to already growing concerns about possible legal action by parents of children in Dupris' class. "It was just a really different experience for the kids so they didn't really get to talk a whole lot and to process it."

Dupris declined an opportunity to comment.

Schultz, like other Peter Hobart parents, praised Principal Shelly Nielsen.

"I think she was incredibly focused on Penny and Sarah and what they needed. They had a lot to deal with too," said Schultz. "But she (Nielsen) also went above and beyond for the students and families, sometimes maybe more than she was advised to."

Schultz also noted that the St. Louis Park District did make great efforts to make sure that all students who had been on the Lilydale Park field trip had access to professional help, if requested. Budget cuts have since made large dents in that resource.

Yet, after the May 22, 2013 event the District spared no cost. Grief counselors and support staff from nearby Park Nicollet Hospital were a huge help, according to all accounts. Perhaps just as important were the specially-trained therapy dogs from Paws For Learning that came to the school every day.

"I've seen firsthand the healing power of the hands-on touch and the unconditional love that only a dog can give to ease pain," said Lund.

The psychological impacts of the tragedy clearly varied

among the fourth graders.

"It's a funny age because some of them can really comprehend and some aren't developmentally at that level yet," concluded Reise, who had a fourth grade daughter and was very active in the PTO. "I think that some of the kids had some real existential questions. But I did observe differences."

Survivor's guilt could have been a factor among children facing unanswerable questions about why Mohamed, Haysem and others had been buried in the hillside collapse that day, while other students were unharmed.

"Some people talk about differences between people who were up the hill or down," said Sandy Boettcher, referring to those who were in the ravine when the Lilydale Park landslide happened. One of those was her son Shane who was among other fossil-hunters from the group who were nearby. "I think there's some truth to that although it certainly affected everyone."

The Peter Hobart school atmosphere was quiet or even somber for the rest of May. That was especially unusual for the end of a school year.

"You would walk in and think the school was closed. ...You'd watch the kids out on the playground at recess and they weren't playing the way they usually would," recalled Lund. "The kids that were on the field trip together and their friends were clumped together talking quietly or maybe not even talking."

Trauma and death clearly had impact. A secular institution, the school was at times as quiet as places generally associated with religious faith.

"It was pretty somber, especially among the fourth graders," agreed Reise. "I think it wasn't until the next-to-last day of school when they all got to go to a bowling alley when I saw them having fun and really being kids again."

It was a lighthearted event that school staff wisely scheduled to help change the atmosphere. But the effects of the landslide wouldn't end that easily for all the impacted students. Some would need further counseling and suffer symptoms of post-traumatic stress for years. Many had nightmares or were especially frightened by lightning storms or other loud noises.

"You may think that they always bounce back," said Schultz. "But I'll tell you that the older they get each year and they become more aware of the world and how it works, the impact it is having on them. ...Those kids are not done with that yet."

Parents reported emotional flashbacks triggered years later by a variety of situations. It might be a TV news story including pictures of Mohamed and Haysem on the screen. It might be walking near a bluff in a park area. Or it could be other events normally considered harmless aspects of the Minnesota good life.

Lund described how her daughter years later was on a family trip to a northern Minnesota cabin and became greatly disturbed by the crashing sounds of trees being cut down in the woods.

"She just started crying and crying. She said she didn't know why and was apologizing," recalled the mother. "I said it's OK, Bella. I do. I do."

Parents and other adults also sometimes experienced

stress or guilt after the event, particularly with their inability to protect the children who had gone on the fossil-hunting trip.

"That was the first time, the very first field trip I hadn't gone on a field trip with Bella," said Lund. "I still feel guilty even though I know there is nothing I could have done about it. But you carry it with you."

Sandy Boettcher also normally went on field trips that included her fourth-grade daughter, Melissa. But she chose to give her place on the Lilydale Park outing to her college-age son Shane, who had been volunteering at Peter Hobart and had shown great interest in becoming an elementary school teacher. He would be at the exact scene of the landslide, thrown into heroic efforts to dig out student Devin Meldahl by hand, while worrying about the status of his younger sister (and vice versa).

She was unharmed. But it was an extremely stressful experience that would have lasting impacts for Shane, as it would anyone in that situation.

"That has continued to affect him, even if he won't talk about it much. ... He'll sometimes say he wishes he could have done more. Maybe if he'd have dug harder or faster he'd have saved somebody else, he thinks sometimes," said Sandy of her son. "But I try to tell him he did all he could and there definitely was a reason he was there instead of me. He was young and athletic and could do more physically, run up and down those hills. I don't know if Sarah could have dug out Devin by herself. Everyone did all they could."

Teachers undoubtedly also had to carry a heavy burden – all the way to the present. But legal and emotional concerns have seemingly muzzled their public comments, if not personal feelings.

"I've seen how it has affected the principal and the teachers," observed Bassin. "I know it has really affected all the people involved. … It was life changing for a lot of people."

The only known public quote from a teacher was from an environmental science teacher who wasn't on the field trip but had taught many of the Peter Hobart fourth graders. Pat Hartman told the Echo, the St. Louis Park high school newspaper how they were his greatest concern.

"I keep thinking about the kids. They didn't know how to react to it," said Hartman. "But I know these kids and they are resilient and are going to pull through."

That kind of faith represented a certain confidence and hope that would help hold together the entire Peter Hobart and St. Louis Park communities. But they would face those challenges for some time, along with outside scrutiny and potentially divisive forces.

Peter Hobart Elementary became an impromptu memorial site after the landslide, drawing well-wishers and media. Students and teachers struggling to deal with the impacts of the tragedy were visited by dignitaries such as Minnesota Gov. Mark Dayton. (below.) But the pain didn't end.

Lilydale Park neighbors also grieved after the landslide. But the most lasting impact was the closure of the entire bluff area that has continued to the present. Orange fencing would eventually be replaced, but city promises of resolving erosion and safety issues have still not been entirely fulfilled.

Saint Paul Mayor Chris Coleman (above) and Parks & Recreation Director Mike Hahm (left)

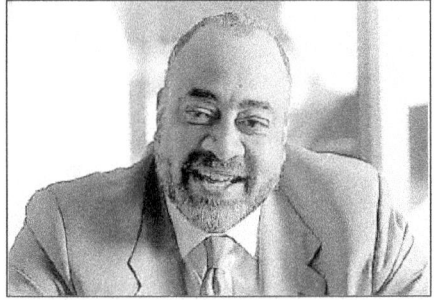

Lancine and Maduso (above) visit Mohamed's gravesite in Burnsville, MN. There has never been any kind of memorial to him, Haysem or any acknowledgement of the May 22, 2013 landslide in Saint Paul. There have however been other unrelated memorials since purchased & placed on park property (below) within very short distance of the accident site.

City officials pivoted quickly in the face of questions about the Lilydale Park tragedy hiring former Hamline Univ. Law dean Donald Lewis (top) and an engineering firm to produce an "independent" investigation. Neither would ever look closely at impacts from a major storm-water culvert expansion & unplugging project (schematic above) that was completed just before the landslide.

Chapter 6

When the night has come
And the land is dark
And the moon is the only light we'll see
No I won't be afraid, no I won't be afraid
Just as long as you stand, stand by me

– Ben E. King

"Loyalty to the country always. Loyalty to the government
when it deserves it."

– **Mark Twain**

The Fofanas were understandably too preoccupied with funeral arrangements and their own needs in response to the Lilydale Park tragedy to attend either the press conference or Gov. Dayton's visit to Peter Hobart. At least one family friend did attend, but was unimpressed by the lineup of political figures' speeches to the assembled students.

'It wasn't about honoring the boys, it was about putting on a show," said Andrea Cloud, noting how emotionally stressed Mohamed's parents were at the time. "I'm glad the Fofanas weren't there."

They had made themselves incredibly available to reporters even during the hours and days immediately following their son's death. But occasionally intrusive media and other public attention, along with the unclear circumstances of the landslide, could have made anyone wary or suspicious. The other two families most affected by the catastrophe would soon largely back away from the public eye, and even other Peter Hobart parents.

However, there was never any doubt that Mohamed's parents had the backs of school staff. The Fofanas never joined in questioning the school's decision to continue with the fossil-hunting trip despite the recent rains. Nor did they question that their son had benefited from his time and experiences at Peter Hobart.

"We always knew the school really cared about him (Mohamed). If the school knew it was dangerous they wouldn't have taken them there," said Lancine confidently, with Madosu nodding in agreement.

Their two younger sons, twins Hassan and Al-Seny were still students at Peter Hobart and the family had strong connections they were determined to keep. Serious tests would follow, but even in the darkest hours after the landslide, it became clear that a special relationship had been born from the tragic deaths.

"Mohamed is gone. But God has given me 47 more kids," Lancine concluded, referring to the remaining fourth graders who had been on the ill-fated field trip.

Peter Hobart Elementary staff also did their best to stay connected. On the evening of May 23, 2018, just hours after Mohamed's body was found, Principal Shelley Nielsen went directly to the Fofanas' home to share her condolences and that of the entire school.

"I was a little surprised," admitted Lancine of the gesture. "But it showed they really cared. Everybody was crying. We became like one, those days. ...It was time for us to stand together and reduce the pain. ...That bond between us and them we will always have."

At the Fofanas' request, Nielsen returned to their house shortly thereafter along with Mohamed's fourth grade teacher, Sarah Reichart.

"Sarah was kind of scared," remembered Lancine. "So Madosu and I went up and put our arms around her. We told her we were all in pain but we would get through this together. She was now part of our family."

Rather than possibly blaming Reichart or other Peter Hobart staff for Mohamed's death in Lilydale Park, the Fofanas focused on the positive. It was the beginning of a special relationship that continues to the present.

"Sarah came over to our house every day, every day. She cared about Mohamed so much," added Lancine, noting that Reichart had already done special tutoring with their son before the accident. "We lost a son but gained a sister."

It certainly wasn't that the Fofanas lacked for blood family and other support during those days immediately after the landslide tragedy. Visitors at their home and well-attended public ceremonies kept them almost constantly busy.

Following Muslim tradition, Mohamed was buried Saturday – just three days after his death – washed and shrouded but without a coffin. Following a service at the Dar Al Farooq mosque in Bloomington, nearly 500 people came to the Garden of Eden cemetery in nearby Burnsville. Men gathered at the graveside while women stood a short distance away – again according to tradition.

"It was very interesting because Guinean men are not supposed to show emotions, especially at funerals," said Cloud, based on her experience in Africa. "But grown men were balling their eyes out (at Mohamed's burial). That shocked me and spoke to the peoples' anguish about this."

Mohamed's grave site marker, like most in the Islamic cemetery, is a simple brass plate in the ground. It bears his name, birth and death dates, and a crescent symbol. Facing to the east, towards Mecca, it is part of a bucolic scene overlooking the Minnesota River valley.

The 10-year-old's death and its continuing impact on all of Minnesota was again made clear, June 9, at a memorial service that was even better attended than the funeral. A standing-room only gathering at East Side Neighborhood Services in Minneapolis included a variety of dignitaries. Gov. Mark Dayton and Saint Paul Mayor Chris Coleman were among them. Coleman was generously invited by Imam Dukaly to speak at the service. It was another family thank-you for the heroic, if hopeless, efforts of the city's first responders to save Mohamed.

There was, at this time, still little discussion in the Guinean community about responsibility for the landslide deaths.

"As a Muslim they teach us don't accuse anyone," explained Kamar Magassoub, a friend of Lancine's since childhood. "It is God who decides what day we die."

Attention that day was rightfully focused on a fourth-grader whose life and death was bringing together diverse peoples. The memorial was attended by Lancine's co-workers at the SuperValu warehouse and Mohamed's classmates, along with many of the parents and family members, from Peter Hobart School. There were other well-wishers from around the state who came to the service or sent good wishes.

"It was hard to even find parking. So many people came up to us that we never even knew, we were amazed," remembered Lancine. " I told Madosu, you see a lot of people die and nobody even knows or cares about it. God works in mysterious ways. He made this boy, big. From here all the way to Africa, people had memorials for him. Maybe there was a reason."

Finding semi-mystical connections between remembrances for Mohamed across the globe in Guinea and Liberia as well as in the Twin Cities might seem extreme. Yet there is little doubt that the Minneapolis memorial had a profound spiritual impact on many in the audience. Peter Hobart parents were deeply impressed by the welcoming atmosphere of, not only the Fofanas, but the Guinean community members hosting the event and a dinner afterwards.

Alana Bassin noted how Madosu, in particular, led the way in welcoming the large number of St. Louis Park residents even while dealing with her own raw emotions.

"She was sobbing and yet being so helpful to all of us," said Bassin of Mohamed's mother. "The Muslim community in general were so welcoming to Christians and Jews and all the white people there. ... It was a real, inclusive, healing experience."

Others had similar reactions.

"It was really incredible how generous and receptive they were. I know a lot of us had never been to a mosque before and didn't know how to dress or act," admitted Stacy Atlas, another parent of a Peter Hobart student. "It was a great learning experience for adults and kids. It was especially amazing to see their faith and generosity."

All members of the Islamic community appeared glad to break bread with their Christian and Jewish guests.

"I don't think I've ever eaten food like that before. It was a great experience with such welcoming people," agreed Andraya Lund. "Especially in this time when we see so much social and cultural bias, to interact with the Muslim community like that was just incredible."

Especially incredible, she added, were the Fofanas. They could understandably have been totally consumed with their own loss. Yet they somehow found time and energy to lead the welcoming of the Peter Hobart school community and other guests to Mohamed's memorial service.

"I will be forever grateful to the Fofana family for the the graciousness and love they showed all of us. I have no words," said Lund.

"They are some of the most incredible, giving people I've ever met," seconded Atlas. "Every situation, while they were still grieving, they were looking out for others."

The Fofanas, characteristically, expressed surprise at hearing the praise directed at them.

"We were not heroes. This is part of Islam. You have to welcome everyone. We treat everybody as same people because we are all feeling the same pain. ...Mohamed was not just for us. He was for everybody," said Lancine with humility. "And seeing all those people gave us energy. The support was big."

The positive energy clearly flowed two-ways.

"I didn't know much about the Muslim religion. I didn't

really even know them (the Fofanas) before the memorial service. But they were just so open and welcoming and humble at such a time," said visiting parent Sandy Boettscher. "They're an inspiration. They're the kind of people you want in your life. ...I give them most of the credit for how they helped bring together the whole community after that."

Certainly the Fofanas set a great and continuing example for everyone.

But St. Louis Park and Peter Hobart School community members were already creating their own impressive and generous response to the victims of the Lilydale Park landslide. Almost immediately, leaders of the PTO decided that all proceeds of their 2013 annual Spring Family Fun Night fundraising event would be donated to the families most impacted by the catastrophe.

Then they upped the ante by adding a special on-line auction in conjunction with local business owner Tammy Cabrera, who was also the parent of a Peter Hobart fourth grader. Her Muddy Paws Cheesecake business became temporary headquarters for a drive that aimed to raise $20,000 to $30,000 by June 5. To everyone's surprise, they eventually raised approximately double that amount. She and PTO volunteers worked overtime to handle a deluge of public response.

"That whole first week we were running like 20 hour days," remembered Lund. "Actually it was just part of the madness that had started and it didn't end for a month (after the May 22, 2013 incident). We were either at the bakery (Muddy Paws Cheesecake) or at the school."

The fundraising part of the madness was generally very

positive, with people and businesses calling and coming in with donations. Then the volume of bids almost overloaded volunteers auctioning 130 items ranging from Vikings football tickets to washing machines, to gift baskets – and, of course, cheesecakes. Phone calls, emails and walk-in pledges came in unexpected numbers and amounts.

There were a number of other spin-offs. The PTO supported a clothing drive for the families, with some donations eventually going to school children in Guinea, Africa as well.

But the biggest beneficiaries might have been the parents, teachers and others in the Peter Hobart school community who were struggling with the aftershock impacts of the Lilydale Park fossil-hunting horror.

"I and others really threw myself into the Fun Night. That was probably my coping. It was therapeutic," said Atlas.

"It was just wonderful seeing the outpouring of support from all over the metro and people contacting us with offers," remembered Derek Burrows Reise, another of the main organizers. "Managing it all coming in was the biggest challenge. ... But it was just so very positive. That made me feel like I was part of a real, caring community. People made things happen without barriers.

"You feel very powerless as a parent especially," he added. "The power of doing something constructive was a relief."

Lund agreed, describing the event as having the additional benefits of both temporarily distracting from the pain and reminding her of the potential goodness of humans.

"I had people I hadn't physically seen for 25 years and even strangers coming up and offering to help. We had more items than we knew what to do with," she said, describing getting a quilt that had been anonymously sent from Duluth. "That was one of those beautiful moments where people really stood up."

Inspirational moments were badly needed at that time in St. Louis Park. Atlas described another at the Spring Family Fun Night when Lancine unexpectedly showed up to show his appreciation for the community support.

"I didn't know what to say to him. I still regret it," she recalled, referring to the fresh, raw emotions felt at the appearance of the deceased fourth-grader's father. "But then kids came running up and encircled him and saved the day. They didn't worry about social differences or niceties. Kids just knew he was related to their friend Mohamed, and that was all that mattered."

The deep wounds caused by the Lilydale Park landslide were not going to be so easily healed for everyone, however.

Understandably confused and pained by the inadequately explained injuries and deaths, the parents of Devin Meldahl and Haysem Sani largely withdrew from Peter Hobart community events and connections. They were increasingly critical of the school's decision to have allowed the field trip to go forward. In mid-July, they would break media silence to tell their stories on local KARE-TV and Minnesota Public Radio.

Devin's mother, Danielle, first described on camera how her son had been buried alive – suffering two collapsed lungs, a fractured skull, broken ribs and a broken leg. They were without health insurance and, despite sharing part of the PTO funds, they had accumulated nearly $100,000 in medical bills during Devin's week-long hospital stay.

She then directly criticized fossil trip leaders from Peter Hobart for not explicitly telling parents of all dangerous conditions in Lilydale Park.

"They should have consulted with us and let us know: The area's not a very safe area. There's caves. There's cliffs. Are you OK with us taking your child down there?" Danielle told reporters. "I don't think I would have let Devin go if I knew the situation."

Haysem's father, Mohamed Muse was equally harsh. He had initially thanked rescue personnel who found his son's lifeless body. But his reactions changed when four days after the incident, he decided to hike around police barriers to see the landslide location for himself. Based on what he saw, and without further background information, the bereaved father grew suspicious - particularly toward school officials.

"This is a dangerous place," he said, describing a sharp cliff above and rocks below where Haysem and Mohamed were buried in the landslide. He also described seeing a shovel left behind by emergency responders. "How they going to bring the kids here?"

Interestingly, neither of the parents directed blame at Saint Paul officials responsible for maintaining Lilydale Park and its public safety. Meldahl and her son would, ironically, soon move into the city where the tragedy occurred. They couldn't be reached for comment more recently, but their harsh words had lasting impacts for school officials.

"Criticism from the families was very hard for all of us to hear," said Sara Thompson, St. Louis Park School District communications director, noting that they did change their parental permission slip process after the event. New slips make information about any risk on any field trip more explicit. "We too learned from it and listened to parents."

But she nevertheless defended the basic decisions made by teachers and administrators who had been involved with the ill-fated field trip.

"It was incredibly hard for the school principal and all the teachers involved. But we gained strength through going back to our core values of caring about the children and our community," she said. "We believed we were taking our students to a safe place that day. It was heartbreaking for all of us."

Off-camera, Muse expressed even stronger criticisms of Peter Hobart officials, according to Lancine Fofana. He feels Muse's angry words may have played a role in teachers and others in St. Louis Park Schools' increased hesitation to publicly discuss the catastrophe.

"He (Muse) said you know the school killed our kids, two black Muslim boys," remembered Lancine, referring to both his son, Mohamed, and to Haysem – whose family were Oromo, originally from Ethiopia. "We said no, we don't believe that and it won't bring our kids back. But he was always angry. So we cut communication."

Connections would be sadly similarly lost between Haysem's family and other Peter Hobart parents and staff.

"Devin was really a good kid, lots of fun," said Atlas, who as a volunteer helped tutor him in fourth grade. "And I know Haysem was really well-liked too, and really bright. ...It was too bad that the other kids really didn't get to say goodbye to him the way they did Mohamed."

The Fofanas would soon be approached by, and would join with, the other families affected by the Lilydale Park landslide in looking at their legal options.

But even after conferring with attorneys and their investigators about responsibilities for their son's death, they would remain loyal to school staff. They had chosen the special St. Louis Park program for Mohamed, and later their two other sons, after trying out other schools nearer their North Minneapolis home. The internationally themed education and the general openness of administration and teachers had been particularly appreciated. It wasn't something they would easily forget.

"I never blamed the school. ... Zero," again said Lancine with conviction. "The school cared for our kids. They cared for their knowledge. ...We knew they would never do something dangerous (that) they knew about."

Criticism of Peter Hobart school teachers and officials for approving the field trip to Lilydale Park nevertheless continued in some quarters, including the media. The District's decision to discourage public comment by employees was perhaps understandable as a legal strategy. But it left the public conversation largely one-sided at a key time.

"There's never enough communication," said Thompson. "Should we have done more? Always. But we were doing our best."

A siege mentality of a sort also set in with some Peter Hobart parents. They remember feeling both disappointment at the lack of information from District officials, and also being wary of media who were pushing for information about the landslide and reactions. Some families described repeated phone calls from reporters and overly aggressive efforts from TV crews in particular.

"Parents and teachers were very protective of kids. It felt very violating," said Reise. "I think most of the people didn't blame the school itself. ...Most of their criticism was about them getting out information sometimes. But even then I think people understood how little information they had and the legal situation."

It was a dilemma, to be sure, for St. Louis Park School District officials.

"They just shut down on lawyers' advice," agreed Lund, the PTO Chair. "To a certain degree I understand that. But then a lot of the parents were coming to me for answers and I didn't have a lot."

Bassin, who happened to be a lawyer specializing in risk assessment, spoke up publicly for the Peter Hobart teachers in a June 6, 2013 *StarTribune* commentary. More recently she continued to argue that fingers were being pointed in the wrong direction.

"I thought it was sensationalist journalism," said Bassin, referring to criticisms of school staff. "I don't think a school has any responsibility to check the safety of a public park and to see if land is caving in. ... If you don't have the reports or information studies you can't possibly know or be able to foresee something like that."

That perspective, however, was surprisingly absent in

most public discussion.

Certainly few in media were questioning the City of Saint Paul's curious inability to foresee problems in Lilydale Park despite repeated warnings. Most reporters dutifully accepted city arguments that the 2009 consultant report calling for detailed study of all ravine erosion in bluff areas somehow didn't apply to the east clay pit area where the landslide occurred. Others quickly complied with the Coleman Administration's refusal to discuss safety issues until after Northern Technologies Inc. delivered its "independent" report – commissioned and paid for by the city.

A rare exception was Tim Blotz of Fox 9 News, who actually spent time looking at background information and doing homework on the history of Lilydale Park issues. We arranged to take a walk through the area while an accompanying cameraman shot clear and dramatic video of the 2011 landslide site, just 75 yards from the location of the 2013 tragedy. It made clear the obvious warning signs that Saint Paul officials had ignored.

Blotz's June 23 televised commentary again pointed to the city's 2009 consultant report calling for an erosion inventory of the entirety of Lilydale Park costing between $11,000 and $15,000. Brad Meyer from Saint Paul Parks and Recreation acknowledged on camera in 2013 that the study was never done.

"It's something that we didn't see an immediate cause for concern. So within the certain window of time we felt comfortable that we'd be able to take a closer look at it. And we just haven't gotten to that point yet," he said shamelessly.

Blotz's report concluded with University of Minnesota soil researcher Prof. Satish Gupta stating his professional opinion that, at the very least, some kind of survey should have been done.

"If there's some problem that it's going to cause some failure and some lives are going to be lost, it's very, very important," Gupta said. "If it's a public area that they should be doing that kind of survey so if that slope is going to fail that they should kind of barricade the area to prevent the people from going in there right after the rain falls."

Amazingly the piece got no followup attention from other media, by now having moved on to summer barbecue and lake cabin stories. But it did get the attention of Saint Paul officials, as reflected in a flurry of nervous email exchanges noting their "depressed" reactions to the Channel 9 piece.

Even less publicly, there had been other stirrings the city could not ignore.

A major law firm had taken on representation for families for the dead and injured children in the landslide. Investigators for Schweibel, Goetz and Sieben would visit the site and quickly conclude there was probable basis to challenge the city's claims of having no liability. They made that conclusion despite Minnesota state statutes which limited legal payouts in public park accidents to $1.5 million total for all claims. It was legislation that clearly gave the City of Saint Paul significant protection and leverage in lawsuits.

Indeed, Minnesota Statute §466.03 subd. 6e even granted governmental entities general immunity from claims "based upon the construction, operation, or maintenance of any property owned or leased by the municipality that is intended or permitted to be used as a park, as an open area for recreational purposes, or for the provision of recreational services."

The only exception to this recreational immunity provision noted that governmental entities are still liable for conduct that would entitle a trespasser to damages against a private person.

This strange-sounding standard still gave burden-of-proof advantage to the city. To win a claim, the Fofanas and the other Peter Hobart field trip families would have to establish that the city had known, or should have known, that any trespassers (or fossil-seekers in this case) could have faced bodily harm from an artificial condition in Lilydale Park.

Even then, the law required proof that: 1. The condition: a: is one which the possessor (City of Saint Paul Parks and Recreation) has created or maintained, and 7 b: is, to (City of Saint Paul Parks and Recreation) knowledge, likely to cause death or serious bodily harm to such trespassers, and c: is of such a nature that (City of Saint Paul Parks and Recreation) has reason to believe that such trespassers will not discover it, and 2. The possessor (City of Saint Paul Parks and Recreation) has failed to exercise reasonable care to warn such trespassers of the condition and the risk involved.

It was a series of very high statutory standards that must have given pause to Schweibel, Goetz and Sieben before taking, on a contingency basis, a case representing relatively low-income families. Only rarely have plaintiffs succeeded, with many failures recorded including an even more recent Stillwater Minnesota case involving a child swimmer's death from a rare parasite found in a public body of water ironically named Lily Lake. While Minnesota torts refer to an assumedly lesser standard for child "trespassers," case law has thus far only applied the more difficult adult standard.

Saint Paul's legally-trained minds, including Mayor Coleman, must have already assessed their statutory advantage as well as other obvious advantages in legal resources including a full City Attorney's Office powered by taxpayer dollars. But in the court of public opinion, the odds were more likely to even out as more questions began to arise.

Once again the city concluded that the best defense was a good offense.

Just before the Blotz' video was scheduled to run on June 21, the city announced it was hiring a second and lead "independent" investigator, Donald M. Lewis. He was a familiar and trusted face to a number of City Hall insiders, as well as bearing the credentials of being dean of Hamline University School of Law. That he was leaving that position with closing of the law school and looking for work at his reopened private practice, was little noted.

"The City of Saint Paul is committed to getting to the bottom of what happened on that tragic day," claimed Coleman's office in a press release. "Don's resume speaks for itself. He is a person of the utmost integrity and his reputation is beyond reproach. I have full faith that he will conduct this independent investigation in a robust and thorough manner. The families of Mohammed (sic) and

Haysem deserve nothing less."

Coleman spokesperson Joe Campbell would explain to a Pioneer Press reporter that Lewis would particularly focus on an internal review of city policies and processes. That had begun after the landslide just as it would after any major event, maintained Campbell. But officials had purportedly decided to hire Lewis because of how complicated the effort was to look at all the emails and records.

Interestingly, among the emails were several sent out by Saint Paul Emergency Management director Rick Larkin. He was still seeking to set up the already-delayed After Action Review process for heads of all city departments involved in the incident.

Larkin pitched hard. He noted that commitments had been made to each other and city emergency responders to hold what was a normal AAR for any event, but especially for one of Saint Paul's largest emergency responses ever.

"As Director, I believe this effort is important – not for what it might tell us about this event. It is critically important, so we can address those areas that need improvement and sustain those areas that worked well, **for the next event!** (emphasis in original.) To keep our people safe and provide excellent service," wrote Larkin.

Interestingly, the email chain appeared to end with only one response – from Saint Paul Parks and Recreation Director Mike Hahm. "Should this be postponed until the investigation concludes?"

The AAR was never conducted and Lewis' investigation would choose not to look at any actual events that happened on the day of Mohamed and Haysem's deaths.

With Lilydale Park remaining officially closed and media dutifully waiting for the city's commissioned "independent" studies to conclude at an undetermined time, the landslide incident began to finally move somewhat out of the public eye.

It was undoubtedly a welcome respite for many. Bewildered Saint Paulites were torn between trust in their public officials and unanswered questions about how one of the parks in America's Most Livable City had become a world-renowned death trap. Peter Hobart School community members were struggling with their own close-to-home issues and psychic wounds that needed healing.

But the summer break couldn't end the impacts of an event that was bigger than individual concerns. Like the eye of a hurricane, the whirlwind of May 22, 2013 would return.

"It got quiet for awhile," remembered Lund. "Then after the investigation it got creepy again."

Chapter 7

"The five stages of bureaucratic grieving are: denial, anger, committee meetings, scapegoating, and cover-up."
— **Charles Stross, _The Rhesus Chart_**

Through their own words
They will be exposed
They've got a severe case of
The emperor's new clothes

-- Sinead O'Connor, The Emperor's New Clothes

It was a well choreographed event, as it should have been after weeks of planning. Mayor Chris Coleman's administration wasn't going to let a landslide bury their political future.

Coleman took the podium first on September 5, 2013 with talking points in hand. Drafted by mayor's office communications director Joe Campbell, they were refined by consultations with a D.C. based political message consulting organization, and approved by City Attorney Sara Grewing. Saint Paul's mayor, and would-be Minnesota Governor, was well prepared to sell the city's story line regarding the deaths of Mohamed and Haysem in Lilydale Park.

He would tell the gathered TV, radio and print media that his office had been focused for three months on finding truth, especially because of their sympathy with all the parents and families of students on the Peter

Hobart Elementary School field trip. Coleman then claimed, with a straight face, that the city had done everything in its power to investigate the landslide.

"My heart goes out to the parents and families of Mohamed and Haysem and others hurt or impacted by the May 22nd landslide," he concluded. Coleman would also announce that the city was undertaking an evaluation of "protocol" in Lilydale Park operations – again including a potential partnership with the Minnesota Department of Natural Resources among others.

But he made no commitments to add signage or common-sense public education measures addressing dangers near the bluff areas during rainy periods. There was no defined period of time nor any clear goals for Lilydale Park safety improvements other than "making it more clear the inherent risks of entering a natural, un-managed park area."

Coleman would also charmingly describe his ongoing support for youth experiences in the natural world. He pointed to his recent camping trip with a group of teens to Glacier National Park. He did not mention the inner-city youth camping program the Friends of Lilydale Park had initiated, but Saint Paul Parks and Recreation had abandoned.

The Mayor's sincerity can only be measured against the quality of the official reports his administration commissioned. His intro made clear what direction that would turn. With that, Coleman turned the podium over to that day's headliner act, Don Lewis.

The James Earl Jonesesque former law school dean and assistant federal prosecutor had been hired by the city at a cost of over $136,000. He would be followed by a spokesperson for NTI, which was paid another approximately $100,000 by the city for their brief work. It was a well-scripted one-two punch.

Perhaps for further distraction, a National Parks Service official came forward to describe how his agency could potentially offer helpful insights into management of Mississippi River areas like Lilydale Park.

Lewis' presentation was given out in the form of an official-looking three-inch thick, bound "study." It was really only 35 pages, but tacked on were 437 pages of attachments that included multiple weather reports and outdated Saint Paul Parks and Recreation Department documents.

Some truly interesting emails and photos were thrown in at the end. But they came in confusing order with almost no context for an average reader. Media was only given all of the information shortly before the press conference began. There was very little time to review or prepare educated questions.

In his baritone voice, Lewis authoritatively described how he and his staff had conducted more than 30 interviews with city staff and community leaders, while pulling together 90,000 emails, 8,037 other electronic files and 22,203 paper files in the course of his investigation. It sounded impressive.

Overlooked, though on the first page, was the investigator's "Scope of Work" that had been contractually negotiated with City Hall. It carefully limited Lewis' investigation to "the City's internal processes, procedures and communications" about soil erosion conditions in Lilydale Park before the children's deaths. Nothing that happened on May 22, 2013 was covered in the report.

Furthermore, the contract with the city specifically ruled out any evaluation of Saint Paul employees or contractors, any determination of the cause of the incident, and any inquiry into the adequacy of emergency response.

In other words, the investigation was effectively designed to limit or entirely avoid any possibility of blame falling on the City of Saint Paul. Lewis may have talked with a number of personnel, yet he was clearly forbidden to press beyond their self-evaluations of judgment or actions regarding public safety.

Essentially unaddressed was the basic question of whether Parks Department or other employees should have reasonably interpreted multiple previous warning signs of bluff collapse as potential dangers to humans. Also unaddressed is whether they had adequately responded to clearly understood problems with storm-water erosion on the bluffs and ravines in Lilydale Park.

Incredibly, the Lewis report did not include any interviews with firefighters, police or 911 personnel – the very people who might best say what went wrong that day and how to prevent it from happening again. Other non-city employed witnesses, with key perspectives, would similarly never even be interviewed including geologists on site the day of the landslide.

My own introduction to Lewis' investigative approach had come in mid-July during a tour of Lilydale Park. One of the first things I showed him was the Cherokee culvert that still had fresh signs of the unplugging work completed by Public Works contractors just before the incident. As we looked into the ravine where storm-water had been sent down the hill into the accident site, he shrugged and mumbled something about how NTI would be looking into all the geology and hydrology questions.

Next we walked to Vento's View overlook, where I pointed out the bluff erosion that in 2006 had led a high level Parks and Rec staff person to demand the building of a wrought-iron fence to keep the public back from the eroding bluff's edge. There was no mention whatsoever in Lewis' report of that clear human safety concern, nor apparently any interview with the former city staffer who still lived in the Twin Cities.

He did take notice of the unmistakable evidence left from the massive 2012 Lilydale Park landslide. Fallen trees and rubble down the entire cliff on what would be called the North Knob could hardly be missed.

But the lawyer was inexplicably more intrigued by finding signs of smaller landslides on the other side of the accident site. Lewis may have already been developing a defense strategy. His report would later emphasize the overall instability of all bluffs in the area – an undeniable but simplistic truth that would somehow become an excuse for city staff's inaction on all safety concerns.

My final striking memory from walking in Lilydale Park with Lewis was his disinterested reaction to a strange, uncannily foretelling experience I had on the Brickyard Trail less than two weeks before the tragic deaths of Mohamed and Haysem. There, roughly 200 yards from the site of the May 22 landslide, I and others had come across two parents - with young children in tow. The adults were both either passed out or nearly incoherent for unclear reasons in the middle of the day. It was a very bizarre and alarming situation.

I called 911, beginning for me a frustrating experience much like that Sarah Reichart would later experience when the landslide came down on the Peter Hobart students. In my conversation too, the Brickyard Trail might as well have been in the Land of Oz as in a Saint Paul park. After 15 minutes of trying to explain the location to a confused operator and urging them to send first responders to the nearby Hwy. 13 entrance, I heard sirens in the opposite direction, well down the hill. I rode my bicycle three quarters of a mile to the Water and Joy Street intersection. There I met and escorted police and fire personnel back up the hill to the troubled family. I left the scene, never hearing an outcome.

My role ended except to describe the event and its example of 911 problems on the Friends of Lilydale Facebook page. Several people responded with similar stories. City Councilman Dave Thune also responded, assuring he would look into repeated problems in emergency response.

Our volunteer group had already informed Parks Director Mike Hahm and department planner Alice Messer of repeated 911 problems that had stretched nearly a decade. They had at least feigned interest, unlike Lewis. He was, it turned out, limited by his contract from looking into the issue.

His real interests were confirmed, at least to me, a few months later. Saint Paul's commissioned top investigator officially concluded that information was "insufficient to enable the City to predict and prevent the deadly slope failure at the East Clay Pit." Lewis faced almost no questioning from reporters about his methods or sources.

NTI followed by offering their own shorter report full of soil-boring and other technical data almost impossible for laypersons, or media, to quickly digest. But inside the report were buried details that suggested similar surprising shortcuts of investigative procedure.

The engineering firm had done only a "limited analysis" of natural and man-made storm-water runoff in the Lilydale Park area. NTI further admitted they did no field surveys nor did they take exact measurements of the ravine where the Cherokee culvert emptied its storm-water and the children were killed in the landslide.

NTI, like Lewis, did not talk with the experienced DNR and Minnesota Geological Society hydrologists who had been on site in Lilydale Park that fateful day. Their investigation ignored other obvious scientific evidence in equally curious ways.

Incredibly, NTI did not make use of free, valuable data readily available from the State of Minnesota. The Department of Natural Resource's topographical survey done in the spring of 2012, using sophisticated LIDAR (laser waves beamed down from an airplane) technology, had scanned the Cherokee Park/Lilydale Park areas. The results showed contours, slopes and distances with a proven high degree of accuracy.

Photos and measurements on a publicly-available DNR website appear to show a much shorter distance than NTI's estimates of a "40-50 width" across the ravine where the landslide occurred. This information alone would appear to undermine their quick dismissal of the possibility that storm-water from the Cherokee culvert might have played a role in the cliff-side collapsing on the school children. But the city-paid engineering firm clearly wasn't ready to seriously study that notion even as they acknowledged its potential.

"Given an estimated velocity of 20 FPS and a drop of 30 feet it is possible for water to occasionally stream as far as the opposite side, but this would occur so infrequently that it is unlikely this contributed to the observed slide," concluded NTI – again, without even measuring the ravine width.

But using their own estimates of water volume and speed running through the 18" metal culvert at the waterfall's edge, a very different, reasonable result can be reached. Using LIDAR estimates of the ravine width as only 20-25 feet, the data suggests storm-water clearly could have shot across the gap during a 10-year rainfall event and likely even a lesser storm.

However, NTI, for reasons that can only be guessed at, would never investigate the possibility. Much like climate change, human impact on Lilydale Park safety was easier to deny if inconvenient science was ignored.

Along with Lewis', the North Dakota engineering firm's official report was largely unchallenged by media gathered at the City Hall press conference. The net effect of the well-choreographed presentation, along with Lewis', was to give seeming legitimacy to Saint Paul's argument, fallacious from the beginning, that the Lilydale Park landslide had been an unpredictable act of nature.

Even if cracks in that cynical explanation had already appeared, the Coleman administration was always able to count on the limitations of the news cycle and attention spans. The city arranged for tours showing selected parts of the now long-closed bluff areas – though certainly not the Cherokee culvert – to help pivot attention in their preferred direction. It generally succeeded.

Headlines and media accounts circulated around the world declaring that an "independent" study had found Saint Paul innocent of responsibility for the two children's deaths. Any analysis usually focused once again on the mysterious, dark and dangerous aspects of Lilydale Park's nature. Few posed any questions about the official line.

Mayor Coleman's PR team had actually been ready for more challenges to the Lewis and NTI reports. Emails gained through the Data Practices Act request show the mayor had been prepped with Q/A exchanges that he must have expected some reporter would initiate. It never happened.

Three of the fictional questions mentioned me by name, something of a curiosity since I hadn't in that time period publicly expressed many of my findings nor had communication with any of the Mayor's staff. But I had offered all my concerns in good faith to Lewis during his "independent" investigation.

Most of the Mayor's prep answers were repetitions of the same theme, now buttressed by the two studies commissioned by City Hall.

"The May 22nd landslide that took the lives of two children and injured two others – was an act of God – an event that the City of Saint Paul could not have predicted or prevented," Coleman's crib notes for the Sept. 5 press conference read. "Had there been indication of an immediate safety risk to park visitors, at this location or elsewhere – park officials and the City would have taken immediate action to secure the area."

As already discussed, that recognition and reaction to obvious safety risks did not officially happen.

But interestingly Saint Paul had on grounds of public safety, long opposed the placement of a statue of Jesus on private property along the nearby West Side neighborhood river bluff. City officials argued very publicly that an unstable bluff meant that Jesus could potentially fall or slide onto passersby below. They only backed off when facing the threat of legal action on First Amendment grounds, shortly before the the 2013 Lilydale Park landslide.

Other clear examples of city employees recognizing public safety dangers from unstable river bluffs included the closing of a popular local bakery on Wabasha Street after a rock slide significantly damaged the building. Similarly, the nearby iconic Green Stairs that provided pedestrian access up and down the West Side bluff had to be totally removed by Public Works as a result of similar concerns.

Lewis's own report noted that after an April 2010 rock slide in Saint Paul's Hidden Falls Regional Park, the area was immediately cordoned off and a geological analysis team was quickly brought in to make certain there was no more danger of slides. Clearly, city staff in those cases had been able to make a connection between bluff erosion and public safety, much as they had when a fence was required at Vento's View in Lilydale Park to address a crumbling bluff line.

Even in the Mayor's simulated press conference where fictional reporters actually asked probing questions, the gap in the city's response logic was sometimes almost comical. One of the Q&As referenced Mike Hahm's earlier statement that Parks "had no reason to believe anything of this nature would occur," despite plenty of evidence to the contrary, including the major 2011 landslide.

The best the city's PR crew could come up with for the mayor's crib notes was to argue that "Mike was saying that no one had any reasons to believe there was an imminent threat to life or injury to persons." In other words, because earlier known landslides hadn't yet killed or injured anyone it was safe to assume they never would. One might ask if such a standard would be accepted if Hahm had a driving accident after being warned by his mechanic that his vehicle's brakes were ready to give out?

Clearly, City Hall was aware of the legal importance of its statements. Emails showed that even basic information, such as NTI's requests to see all written work orders on the Cherokee Culvert, couldn't be handed over to the "independent" investigative firm without first going through Saint Paul City Attorney Sara Grewing.

It is unclear whether NTI received all the information it requested. Their final report suggests they were unable to access basic historical information about city storm sewer locations, which is usually considered vital to municipal utility and public works operations. Some cities have records going back centuries. Curiously, the *Saint Paul Pioneer Press* would request and be able to publish a map of all citywide storm sewer drains in early 2014.

But NTI's report did include a photo of a large section of corrugated metal at the foot of the waterfall near the accident site. "Origins of the pipe are unknown," was the only explanation the engineering firm supplied. Other sections of the sewer pipe were similarly seen throughout the ravine coming from the Cherokee culvert. There was no analysis of their role or the amount of storm-water pressure it would have taken to force them all the way to the landslide site.

Grewing was a particularly key figure in the city's two week preparation period between receiving the Lewis and NTI reports and their public unveiling on September 5. At times Saint Paul's top justice official almost appeared to have joined the Mayor's PR team, leading discussions with top staff on how to spin the results to media.

At one point Grewing delivered a briefing in the mayor's office, using a PowerPoint presentation to indicate how the city's investigations should be pitched publicly to cover shortcomings.

"Investigations did not address anything to do with our response to the incident," she wrote, referring to the limits her own City Attorney's office had helped place in the Lewis contract. "As such, we are saying the NTI report concluded the slide was a natural occurrence, having nothing to do with any manmade activity."

It was another nifty pivot by Saint Paul city leaders. Not that all officials were totally relaxed and confident however   .

The September 5 unveiling of the "independent" investigations culminated a summer of nervous meetings, strategy sessions and consultations. Emails suggest the NTI, and especially the Lewis analyses, clearly put some insiders on edge – ironically even as media and public scrutiny temporarily abated.

The high level of tension among rank-and-file city staff, especially in Parks and Recreation, led several to seek their own legal representation before being interviewed.

Saint Paul Parks and Recreation chief planner Jodi Martinez was clearly worried, evidenced by a June 28 email exchange with her personal attorney regarding an upcoming meeting with Donald Lewis. She particularly noted concerns about photos that had been circulated among city staff, including herself, well over a year before the May 22, 2013 landslide.

"Would be nice to know whether the pictures that Scott Kruse referenced were taken to verify if it was the slide area or one of the other ice climbing areas. If it's the other area, then we may still have a condition that needs looking into ASAP," she fretted, still surprisingly unclear about Lilydale Park's geography.

Martinez' concerns obviously weren't eased after having it confirmed that the photos by a Parks forestry employee, and avid ice climber (Scott Kruse) were definitely of the East Pit area where Mohamed Fofana and Haysem Sani had been killed. Indeed, she quickly sought to distance herself from internal department conversations about the photos which were now in the hands of the "attorney," i.e Lewis.

"My only comment in the email chain was to ask my staff, Alice Messer, to be sure to loop in PW's (Public Works) sewers when she met on site," wrote Martinez,

Parks' lead planner. She concluded by noting, with some apparent relief, that though "my staff" spent nearly 2.5 hours with Lewis, no recording person or device was present.

But the emails from Martinez' city account would be part of the public record along with the referenced email chain. Lewis would even include parts in his report, although mostly in the appendix.

Concern about the underlying photos and other emails that Martinez referenced was understandable. They provided crystal clear prior evidence of city staff knowledge of serious landslide danger in Lilydale Park - even if the Lewis report chose to bury it.

Over a year before the fatal landslide, Kruse had led ice-climbing groups into the same ravine where the Peter Hobart Elementary fossil-hunters would meet with horror. His visits led him to be greatly concerned about continued major erosion in that exact part of the Brickyards area. Photos and email descriptions sent to his Parks department superiors left no doubt about the seriousness of the situation.

Included was Kruse's warning of the possibility of a bluff collapse "in the next year or two. I believe the whole hillside is at high risk to slide in heavy rains," he wrote in a February 1, 2012 email.

To his credit, department supervisor Cy Kosel immediately forwarded Kruse's information and photos to Alice Messer and Ellen Stewart, the lead Parks planners for both the Lilydale Park and Cherokee Regional Trail development projects. They were also among city staff that had received earlier descriptions of landslide events and conditions in Lilydale Park.

"Scott Kruse indicates what we have been noticing for years now, the continued erosion around parts of the clay pits. It would seem that if this continues, it could cause a major slide and affect parts of the upper bluff at Cherokee (maybe not for years, but who knows.)," wrote Kosel.

He then continued by asking another key question. "I was wondering if either of you have ever looked at it for stabilization or for steering away possible sources of water that may be lending to the erosion?"

Bluff instability related to storm water impacts had clearly gotten the attention of top Parks staff, though no positive action would result. A hurriedly arranged tour of the site in February 2012 ended abruptly when Parks supervisor Gary Korum slipped and fell in mud. For some reason that also aborted any serious staff discussion of both environmentally and public safety issues in the area.

Curiously, Korum would later be pressed about the incident by Lewis - but only whether the hike hadn't actually happened earlier, in connection with the 2011 mudslide. The Parks supervisor would even be asked if his fall hadn't happened at another location? The independent investigator's suggestions, if affirmed, could have helped muddy focus on storm-water playing a unique role in the 2013 East Clay Pit landslide.

But Korum refused to go along with Lewis. According to another email, Korum was concerned enough by Lewis' repeated questions about details of his account to suspect he was now being set up as a different kind of fall guy.

Regardless, Kruse's photos and concerns had raised the alarm about Lilydale Park bluff stability and storm-water runoff. It was a particularly timely warning given upcoming city construction plans in the area. Handling of storm water was already a major engineering concern, though not for environmental or public safety reasons.

In an email to top Parks staff, Chief project planner Messer confirmed her own awareness of erosion issues along the bluff even as "we are reconstructing some of the existing catch basins that drain to the bluff."

She was referring to a $120,000 portion of her Cherokee Park trail project, that added asphalt and in other ways was designed to actually increase the flow of storm-water into Lilydale Park. Most of it would come from reconstruction of the nearby 60-inch Cherokee culvert. That project would send runoff from a 50-acre bluff top area directly into the ravine and canyon that would become the site of the fatal landslide. The implications for bluff stability and safety in going ahead with the culvert work should have been obvious.

Messer would go on in her email to acknowledge, "It does seem like the time to address the issue would be in conjunction with the Cherokee Regional Trail project if storm-water run-off from Cherokee is in fact the issue. Of course I have NO MONEY in the Cherokee Regional Trail project to put toward this work..."

There was no further discussion of the issue revealed in city emails that were released in response to my Data Practices request.

Lewis' report offered no hint on whether the matter was brought up in any investigation. It matter-of-factly reported only that Messer had taken a two-hour hike with Public Works engineers around the bluff area after which it was pronounced that no "smoking gun" cause of the erosion was found.

By mid-April, 2012 Messer's email exchanges with the Sewer Division of Saint Paul Public Works were focused on meeting construction schedules. There is no more evidence that the city seriously investigated ways to protect the vulnerable bluff above the Lilydale Park ravine from their own project. The storm-water culvert reconstruction, needed to protect Parks' new asphalt road and trail from pooling rainwater, was clearly the top priority.

Whether this decision played a direct role in the landslide on Peter Hobart Elementary fossil-hunters and sealed the fates of Mohamed and Haysem may perhaps be argued. The passage of time and destruction of evidence, from both more storm water erosion and belated city efforts to control it, makes definitive scientific conclusions impossible.

But there is little question that Saint Paul city officials were, soon after the accident, now privately acknowledging they had a major problem with impacts of storm-water racing through the Cherokee culvert.

On September 5, 2013, the very day that Lewis, NTI and Mayor Coleman stood before the cameras to exonerate the city, Messer sent another email to Martinez. She wrote about a conversation she recently had with a very concerned city engineer. Public Works' recently unplugged, concrete Cherokee culvert was itself being undermined by the volume and speed of storm-water and in danger of being washed downstream into the ravine.

By this time, after the deadly landslide, Messer finally

had a different top priority.

"I told him I was concerned about the larger issue of controlling the amount of water entering the 60-inch pipe and how it is released down the bluff," she wrote. Messer now pushed for a new study to find solutions, noting that the high costs would likely require getting help from neighboring communities, as well as state funding.

Wheels turned quickly. Later that month, Kosel wrote to the DNR, Dakota County and other suburban "partner" communities seeking expertise and financial help in trying to figure out how to make Lilydale Park safe from storm-water impacts. Included in invitations was one sent to DNR hydrologist Dr. Carrie Jennings.

In his opening pitch, Kosel confirmed that city staff realized the major source of problems. He openly admitted that the May 22, 2013 landslide was "directly related to storm-water in combination with unstable bluff soils."

The Cherokee culvert, which would in later studies be found to provide up to 75 percent of all storm-water into Lilydale Park, was now seen as a clear problem bedeviling engineers and park planners all the way to the present.

But publicly, the City of Saint Paul's had already determined the show must go on.

Saint Paul forester Scott Kruse's photos & emails warned of a possible major landslide in the East Clay Pit area well over a year before the tragedy that killed Mohamed & Haysem. Kruse's email to Parks superiors initiated discussion about erosion and an upcoming storm-water project in the same area. Parks planner Alice Messer agreed it would seem to be the time to address the problem. But she said there was no money and then gave the go-ahead to city engineers to continue contracts putting road & asphalt protection over concerns about more water being sent over unstable Lilydale Park bluffs.

"Scott Kruse indicates what we have been noticing for years now, the continued erosion around parts of the clay pits. If would seem that if this continues, it could cause a major slide and affect parts of the upper bluff at Cherokee (maybe not for years, but who knows).
Parks dept. supervisor Cy Kosel email, Feb. 1, 2012

Cherokee Park culvert to Lilydale waterfall / landslide

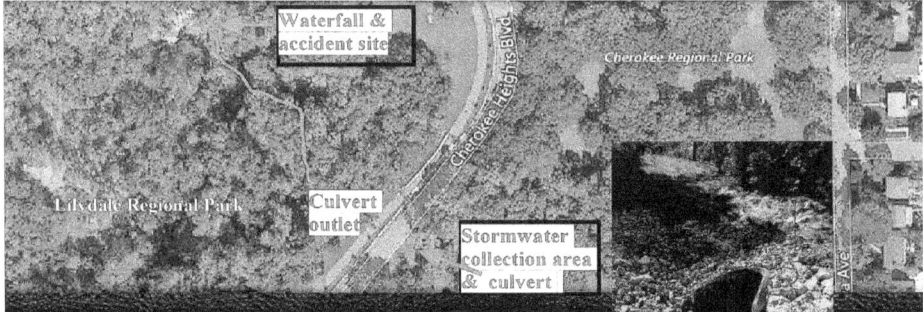

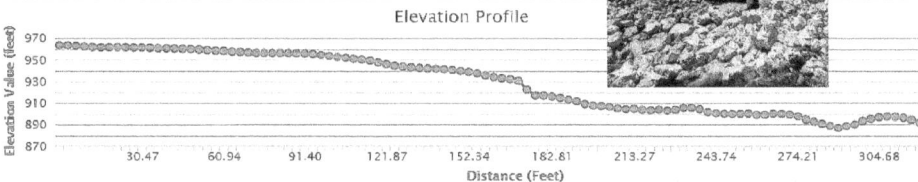

Elevation Profile

Spring 2012 LIDAR survey, MN

Photo 1-3   Erosion and scouring at the outfall of the Cherokee Heights culvert (May 2014 site visit)

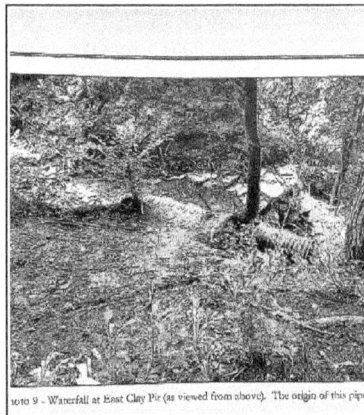

Photo 9 - Waterfall at East Clay Pit (as viewed from above). The origin of this pipe

City engineers and consultants began seeing major erosion impacts from remodelin unplugging of the Cherokee culvert even before NTI's investigation was comp Increased storm-water caused damage all the way down the bluff, with large corru metal pipes found well past the accident site - as even NTI noted.

Chapter 8

"Not everything that is faced can be changed,
but nothing can be changed until it is faced."
-- James Baldwin

D r. Carrie Jennings wasn't entirely forgotten by the Coleman administration. They did include the scientist among recipients of thank you notes from the Mayor sent to all emergency responders who were on site at the May 22, 2013 landslide.

Former Saint Paul Emergency Management Director Rick Larkin has continued to credit her advice with "saving lives" among police and firefighters who were facing falling rock and other dangers that day and the next. Dr. Jennings' recognized expertise, particularly in hydrology, was why she and two other geologists were invited by city officials to the Lilydale Park accident location that day.

So she was surprised that she and the other geologists were never be contacted by Lewis, NTI or other city investigators. In anticipation, the scientist had compiled her own notes and evaluation of the incident for the Minnesota Department of Natural Resources. Coleman had repeatedly and publicly said the state agency would be a lead partner in evaluation of the tragedy and in future planning for making the park safe for fossil groups and other visitors. Dr. Jennings followed protocol in waiting to be consulted.

But she heard nothing from the city until after official investigations were concluded. Saint Paul was by then quietly looking for help with major erosion issues from storm-water flowing through the Cherokee Heights culvert into Lilydale Park. They began reaching out to "partner" organizations and public bodies.

When Park's supervisor Cy Kosel's invitation to a meeting was received, Dr. Jennings responded by including her analysis of the landslide as an attachment. It was likely more information than the city really wanted to hear.

I found Dr. Jennings' analysis in mid-2014, amongst materials sent after a lengthy delay by Saint Paul officials in handling my Minnesota Data Practices Act requests. I was seeking public information to be used in an article I was writing for *City Pages*.

Data Practices requests often involve a dance between the petitioner and the governmental body grudgingly required under law to share information about itself. Officials generally do their best to follow the letter of the law, or the petitioner's request, and nothing more. Burying petitioners in paper is another common tactic. I received multiple paper copies (up to 17 each) from the city of un-requested, unimportant documents such as the Mayor's daily meeting schedules.

But I rarely received any important background materials along with emails that referenced meetings, agendas etc. So when Dr. Jennings' emailed reply to her invitation included her attachments, I knew a gem had slipped through.

Included with materials Dr. Jennings had supplied to the city were her onsite notes and observations from May 22, 2013 along with a critical analysis of the Lewis and NTI investigations. She left little doubt about her opinion of their research and reports. Her own expert observations provided data and devastating details that directly countered their conclusions.

The DNR geologist particularly ripped holes in the city's central argument that the landslide had been precipitated by rainfall that soaked into the sandy topsoil, eventually causing the bluff to slide down on top of the fossil-hunting children. This NTI theory, interestingly, was based on their visit, over a month after the landslide - when it would have been impossible to know the soil saturation on the day of the tragedy.

Dr. Jennings had been in the East Clay Pit that very day working closely with rescue personnel and a crew. Among other tasks, they needed to remove an overhanging tree on the slope above that appeared to be a potential danger to those searching for Mohamed's body. As they pulled and yanked on the tree she watched it release large amounts of sand – "DRY sand," she wrote, onto the canyon below. No signs of soil saturation were seen.

That was only the beginning of Dr. Jennings' observations contradicting the city's case.

She continued by citing Shane Boettcher's group photo taken prior to the accident. Dr. Jennings noted that behind the Peter Hobart students in the shot were already visible clear fractures in the bedrock, located above hollowed-out sandy areas in the canyon walls. When the undermined bedrock could no longer sustain the weight of the bluff above, it cracked and everything fell. To her scientist's eye, it was this unnatural combination which had brought the landslide down on the children.

The cause of the undermining? Dr. Jennings immediately focused on clear visual evidence suggesting unintended consequences of the Cherokee culvert storm-water project.

She also noted several sections of large, broken corrugated metal pipes that had been pushed down the hill over a waterfall onto the accident site. Water had been channeled into the Lilydale Park ravine and then into the canyon where Mohamed and Haysem died. The DNR geologist saw a remaining storm-water pipe, confirmed by a city photo, that was "aimed directly at the rock and sediment face that failed."

Dr. Jennings' suspicions were later independently seconded by Alan Knaeble of the Minnesota Geological Survey, who the day of the landslide also drew a detailed sketch of the canyon area. It prominently noted both broken corrugated metal pieces at the bottom of the ravine, and the remaining pipe at the top pointing toward the wall that collapsed on the children. He observed what appeared to be dramatic impacts from large amounts of water that had been rushing down the hillside.

"Just beyond the mouth of the culvert, the bedrock was totally scoured clean. ...Where that cascaded over the bedrock it came out at the base of the collapsed area and it would be potentially undercutting the shale," he agreed with Dr. Jennings' analysis when contacted by this writer.

Knaeble further noted that the situation that day was different than landslides or "failures" that he had often seen in over two decades of leading fossil groups and others on trips to Lilydale Park.

"Originally when I heard what happened I thought that the (rain) water had collected from the top and seeped through the bedrock causing the failure," he said. "But when we were there, it was obvious it was more than that."

Yet curiously Knaeble was also not contacted nor interviewed by the city's official investigators, who instead relied on the saturated soil theory and NTI's later, limited analysis. Like Dr. Jennings, he had been on the city's master list of persons who had been on-site the day of the landslide.

"I guess, if I was running the investigation I would have thought they'd want to at least talk to all the geologists on site (that day)," Knaeble said, sounding puzzled.

Dr. Jennings had no doubt about why her observations were disregarded by the city. Her written report and comments clearly contradicted the suggestion that Mohamed and Haysem had been killed by an act of God, or an unpredictable natural event.

"I disagree," her email concluded in response to the Lewis and NTI investigation reports. "My hypothesis is that water from the culvert undermined the rock ledge that then collapsed, sending dry material down onto the children."

NTI had summarily dismissed such a possibility.

But interestingly, they included at the end of their report a series of photos that also confirmed the power of the Cherokee culvert storm-water. One prominently displayed the corrugated pipe pointing out from the waterfall area. Others showed more pieces of pipe in the ravine below and other evidence of storm-water velocity, including extensive damage beginning at the culvert's outflow point coming all the way down the hill into Lilydale Park.

For good measure, the NTI engineers threw in photos and schematics of the Cherokee Park culvert reconstruction and unplugging – though they officially insisted it had nothing to do with the accident taking Mohamed and Hassan's lives. It was almost like they were leaving a trail of bread crumbs for anyone following up on their work – as Dr. Jennings did.

The city-hired investigative firm included a photo they described as showing a "freshly cleaved face in the overburdened sands" of the bluff wall. NTI's attempt to evidence their case also included the part of the bluff where the tree had been deliberately pulled down with dry sand as Dr. Jennings described – after the fatal landslide.

But she pointed out an even more fatal evidentiary gap. "What they fail to mention is the rock that fell to let the sand loose," said Dr. Jennings, referring to the undermined shale ledge that had first cracked and precipitated the tragedy.

Indeed, at the bottom of the NTI photo below the bluff can be seen a jagged rock shelf poking out of the sand and debris. Dr. Jennings remembered it well from the day of the tragedy.

"The first responders were asking me to help them estimate how much it might weigh. I gave them the average density of rock and they were thinking about some kind of inflatable device they could place below it and pump up to see if a child was beneath it," she recalled.

Statements and written incident reports by police and fire personnel, though also not included in Lewis or NTI reports, confirm that their rescue efforts encountered large amounts of rocks as well as sand in the accident area. Those on site that day also credited Dr. Jennings' work in helping prevent serious injuries to first responders from falling rocks.

However the highly-respected DNR geologist never got a response from Saint Paul officials to her written analysis of the tragedy. She attended several meetings of the "partners" group that Kosel set up, looking at the Cherokee Heights culvert storm-water issue. But it clearly wasn't a comfortable situation.

"It started being about legal concerns and things. It was pretty clear they didn't really want to hear what I had to say," Dr. Jennings recalled.

That was made more evident after my article "The Shame of Saint Paul" ran in *City Pages* in early November, 2014. Minnesota Public Radio did a follow-up interview with Dr. Jennings, who very articulately confirmed and detailed her dispute with the official investigation.

In response, Saint Paul Parks spokesperson Brad Meyer tried to dismiss Dr. Jennings' professional background and analysis skills in comparison to the NTI and Lewis reports.

"What we have is an in-depth analysis that spans multiple weeks and findings and conclusions that we still stand behind, versus an observation that was maybe a matter of an hour or two either being on site or assessing the situation," Meyer said to the *Saint Paul Pioneer Press*.

For what it's worth, he also told the newspaper – which never bothered to contact Dr. Jennings – that I was "reckless and irresponsible" in my *City Pages* reporting.

Shortly after my article and the MPR piece ran, Dr. Jennings was called into the office of the DNR Commissioner, who had been contacted by the City of Saint Paul. The same state agency that Mayor Coleman had repeatedly referenced as a partner in the Lilydale Park investigation was now being asked to keep its employees quiet about their analysis of the event.

"They were trying to discredit the work," she remembered years later. "I'm grateful that the DNR backed me and stood by the science. But it was a little uncomfortable."

Dr. Jennings was instructed not to speak publicly on the Lilydale Park matter without running it through DNR media offices. It was a moot point as local media had apparently lost all interest and the issue seemingly disappeared from the public eye. No one ever officially followed up on her analysis of the landslide that struck the Peter Hobart Elementary field trip group.

However, Dr. Jennings' landslide expertise has since been welcomed more than ever by her peers at conferences and events throughout the Upper Midwest, and nationally. She has since moved to the Freshwater Society and also heads up an elite statewide survey team helping to create a comparative database and historical record of landslides and erosion incidents throughout Minnesota.

Preliminary results from her project work were part of a 2018 Congressional briefing on the increasing threat of landslides in an age of climate change. The final study is going to be published by the U.S. Geological Survey and is also being closely watched by NASA's international landslide tracking program. Coincidentally, the lead scientist for the NASA program was a student at Peter Hobart Elementary in the early 1990s.

Dahlia Kirschbaum has never been to Lilydale Park, yet her NASA work now takes her all over the world, learning about geologic phenomena that often carry deadly impacts. One recent study estimated that well over 2,000 people are killed each year by landslides. Most experts assume there may well be great under-counting in some parts of the world and that dangers will continue to grow with climate change and increasingly extreme weather events. The Midwest and other flatland areas of the U.S. are generally low on the list of landslide risk, well below places like the Pacific Northwest or Southern California. However, nowhere is immune, as the Lilydale tragedy demonstrated.

Word of the incident involving her elementary school came to Kirschbaum at her NASA office in Northern Virginia, and then in later professional conversations with Dr. Jennings. Like everyone, she was shocked at first. But she had long before concluded that even in places like

Minnesota there needs to be increased awareness of how humans contribute to what are often too-easily called unpredictable natural accidents.

"What I'm learning from events like Lilydale is that landslides are pervasive everywhere," Kirschbaum said, declining to make a judgment on that particular event. "Obviously there are human drivers to landslides, like storm-water. Is there proper retrofitting of sewers, is there knowledge of when slopes are unstable?... What's important is that Minnesota government is making efforts to better monitor and learn to be able to predict landslides."

The success of that effort, however, depends on a willingness to learn from history. Dr. Jennings certainly hasn't forgotten the lessons of the Lilydale Park landslide of May 22, 2013.

"Every time I tell the story of 'why', I almost cry," she said. "It wasn't natural. It was an altered place. It was a mining area and if this had happened in mine spoils on the Iron Range it would have been immediately recognized. The lesson has been learned there."

But Saint Paul had chosen to ignore Lilydale Park's history as a mining area for the Twin City Bricks Company, even as it gave names like "East Clay Pit" to known fossil-hunting areas. Then it added yet another major unnatural feature to the tragic mix, concludes Dr. Jennings.

"You can't discharge storm-water on a slope and then say it's natural," she said with disdain. "That was what the City of Saint Paul promoted – it was an act of God – which is actually an offensive line."

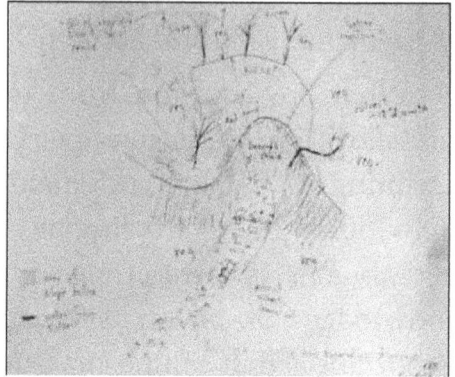

An NTI photo (left) showed the waterfall and a metal pipe above the May 22, 2013 accident site. Geologist Alan Knaeble drew a sketch (above) also showing the pipe, storm-water and pieces of culvert already fallen into the ravine..

Thursday—Sunny and cool

I mapped the surficial geology of Ramsey County for the MGS in 1990 and 1991. I was able to find my field notes and slides of the park that showed the geologic materials. I brought them with me to the site where I was joined by Al Knaeble, MGS and Heather Arends and three engineers from Bolander Engineering. We met St. Paul Public Works personnel in the Mobile Command Center then proceeded to the landslide site. We were able to view it from below and above to assess the stability.

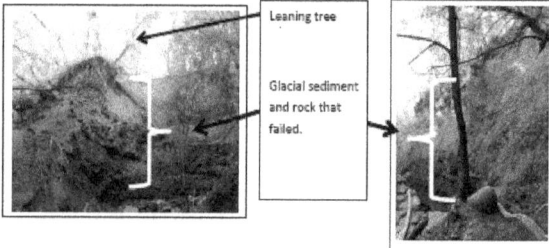

Leaning tree

Glacial sediment and rock that failed.

A significant thickness of the bedrock and the glacial sand and gravel above the bedrock failed. The glacial sand and gravel was of Superior lobe origin and appeared to be filling a small channel in the bedrock surface. Other, older glacial units that were mapped in the park were not preserved here. Younger Superior lobe till and other postglacial units lay above this exposure but were covered and were not involved in the failure.

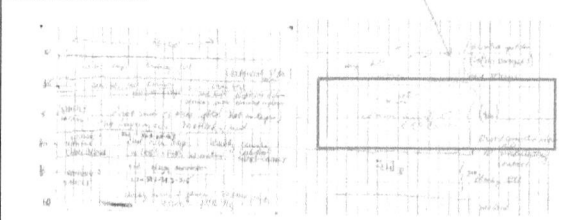

DNR Geologist Carrie Jennings also sketched and photographed the site (left) that day. She noted the pipe at the waterfall was "aimed directly at the rock and sediment face that failed." Jennings further pointed to dry sand on top of the pile to counter the official investigation's claim of ground saturation causing the top-down landslide. Instead, she noted that a "significant thickness" of the supportive bedrock had failed, likely after being undercut by storm water erosion.

******

"When anything happens we look to God first. That is what comes to mind first. That is what makes it easier to handle," explained Lancine of his family's both generous and pragmatic reaction to Mohamed's death.

Yet the Fofanas' intense faith and focus on divine will didn't mean they were unable to assess human responsibility – both positive and negative.

"We could not bring our son back," said Lancine, carefully choosing his words for balance. "But Islam is based on truth. Justice is okay."

The Fofanas continue to seek balance, not bitterness, in their response to Mohamed's death. They have continued to praise emergency workers' efforts to find and save their son, buried under rocks and sand in Lilydale Park. Immediately afterwards they graciously invited Mayor Coleman to speak at Mohamed's memorial service.

But from that point on, the City of Saint Paul's actions, and especially the official investigations, did not impress them as being good faith.

"The city denied it. They said it was all natural. But they know it was not natural," concluded Lancine. "They come out with more than 200 pages (Lewis report) to show they're not guilty. I said it was too much. I can't deal with all of this."

Mohamed's death, along with that of Haysem and the physical and psychological injuries to many others from Peter Hobart Elementary, wasn't ever going to be forgotten however. A legal settlement and payout was the closest thing to justice available to them, even if the city has tried to silence the Fofanas and others from further comment.

"The book (Lewis report) the City put out, we cannot say much. But I knew from the first place that they were wrong and someone had to push them. They have to fix the problem. Forty-nine kids went up there and it could have been any or all of them," Lancine added. "We have to stop this so it will never happen again for other kids."

Families of the other Lilydale Park victims made first contact with attorneys from the respected Minneapolis firm of Schwebel, Goetz and Sieben. Lead attorney John Goetz then contacted the Fofanas and quickly made them aware of their rights, as well as issues that had been difficult for them to see through the pain and chaos of the period immediately after the landslide.

"It was hard for me to talk about it and think about it at first," admitted Madosu. "But he explained everything. Through John we learned a lot of details."

Goetz had taken his own tour of the Lilydale Park accident site, then hired an investigator. They reviewed public data and quickly identified clear advance warnings of danger in the area of the fatal landslide. The city-commissioned Lewis and NTI investigations certainly did not lessen the law firms' belief that they had a strong civil case. City employees' prior knowledge of landslide dangers, revealed in emails, photos and reports only made them more confident. They anticipated that more research would uncover more.

Light did begin to break through in a variety of ways.

About a month after the tragedy that took her son, Madosu made an unrelated, astonishing discovery of her own. It was both sad and uplifting at the same time.

While looking through some of Mohamed's books and school papers, she found a hand-made booklet of drawings and wishes that the 10-year-old had made after his visit with her to Guinea, West Africa two years earlier. The summer break journey had been a major influence on his life plans, as laid out in the booklet. Expressed among his many generous desires was the dream of someday being in a position to "give money so school kids can read."

It was a goal that Goetz pointed out could be realized if the Fofanas, and other families victimized by the landslide, pursued legal compensation from the St. Louis Park School District - and especially from the City of Saint Paul. Out of that conversation the Mohamed's Dream Foundation was born as a concept. Yet, first the sometimes less-than-transparent twists and turns of the American justice system had to be navigated.

Goetz began negotiations with both governmental bodies in hopes of persuading them to recognize their responsibilities without official legal filings and proceedings. Avoiding potential embarrassment before the public eye was the enticement. But, as previously described, strict state legal limits on financial judgments clearly created a strategic advantage for the city and a hurdle for the parents of the Peter Hobart students.

"Generally it is tough to sue municipalities on injuries that occur in public parks," explained Goetz, pointing to the historic English Common Law doctrine of "you can't sue the King." Essentially, it refers to a legal assumption of immunity from claims upon public officials making normal decisions and arguably just doing their jobs. Complainants must be able to show extraordinary circumstances beyond mere bad judgment by "the king's representatives." The notion, while well-meaning, can sometimes place almost impossibly high burdens on plaintiffs.

Other hurdles were more modern and close to home.

"Minnesota juries have gone all over the place on what the death of a child is worth," Goetz added, referring to an unrelated but similar case of a death in a public park. There the victim's family received only $10,000. "That was always in the back of our minds, that kind of outcome."

Nevertheless, the Peter Hobart families' attorneys found other precedent suggesting they had a very winnable case. Their argument was buttressed with an analysis done for them by another respected geologist, University of Minnesota professor Otto Strack. He barely concealed his contempt at the claims of Saint Paul Parks and Recreation officials of having no warning of the dangers in Lilydale Park's bluffs.

"There is no acknowledgment among those responsible for the park that the clay pits are man-made and pose a significant risk to fossil hunters and other visitors," Strack wrote in his analysis.

He was particularly alarmed by the 2011 landslide, about 75 yards from the fatal 2013 event, which he saw as evidence that the city ignored the obvious. "Rather than examining the danger that should have been abundantly clear from the slide, emails and comments indicate a total lack of realistic and responsible assessment of the danger," concluded the geology professor.

On the same day as the release of the Lewis and NTI reports, Goetz contacted Saint Paul City Attorney Sara Grewing with an offer to reach a settlement before giving a formal notice of claim or commencing other litigation. He was obviously unimpressed after his first read of the official reports commissioned by the city.

"Lewis, no, we just thought he was full of shit," Goetz said with a laugh, about the report. He also noted city emails, hidden in the appendix of the report, that contradicted Lewis' basic argument that there was no staff knowledge of dangers before the landslide. "If we had started to sue, we might have found out even more about the geologist (Dr. Carrie Jennings) and things."

If that scenario had played out, it might have placed the City of Saint Paul in even greater legal and financial jeopardy. One exception to strict statutory limits on liability payouts for accidents in public parks revolves around the standard of direct actions by public officials. Where it is established that they or their agents (contractors) are responsible for creating a known hazard, juries can go above the normal $1.5 million in awards to injured parties or families.

Whether the Cherokee culvert work might have constituted such a legal exception will never be known. The role of storm-water in causing the landslide apparently was never a major part of settlement discussions between lawyers for both sides. City officials managed to keep quiet Dr. Jennings' analysis of the ravine where the children were killed until well after all litigation possibilities were concluded.

That settlement happened after several months of behind-the-scenes negotiations between Goetz and Saint Paul attorneys during the fall of 2013. Justice would be defined by dollar signs with both sides focused on the bottom line. It was anything but charitable feelings toward families of the landslide victims that drove the Coleman administration attorneys, especially as discussion of damages grew past the $800,000-$900,000 level.

"We got up to a point in negotiation and it was just really obvious that they didn't like the sound of $1 million from a PR point-of-view or whatever," recalled Goetz.

City officials desperately wanted to avoid the embarrassment of even that relatively modest sum. Plaintiffs' attorneys had some leverage in terms of potential publicity but had to also be aware of the risk of gambling their own and clients' interests against rising court fees and other costs. No one would become rich. Any payout would need to be divided, after commissions, among all four families of the children physically injured or killed by the Lilydale Park landslide.

It was finally agreed in early 2014 to take the matter to a mediator, retired Hennepin County Judge Allan Oleisky. A closed-door, semi-legal hearing and arguments by both sides were heard on January 27. Little is known of the somewhat unusual proceedings except that each side presented material separately to the mediator, with even the victims families kept in separate rooms.

"I was in a fog," said Lancine, acknowledging he could remember little of the proceedings. "To be honest, I didn't really want to be there or to think about money. And for Madosu, every time we had to go to court or see the lawyer it was like Mohamed died again. It was too painful... We just trusted John (Goetz.)"

A Saint Paul City Attorney's Office letter to Judge Oleisky laid out their case. It was apparently based largely on the Lewis and NTI reports, though much of the document was for some reason heavily redacted and cannot be read. It was blacked out when received months later via a Minnesota Data Practices Act request, though all litigation had been concluded and the information is not attorney-client privilege protected. The city has continued, to this day, to limit public access without explanation.

Regardless, the mediation process before Judge Oleisky obviously did not entirely conclude as the Coleman Administration would have liked.

The outcome was a settlement that gave $1 million total to the families of Mohamed Fofana, Haysem Sani and Devin Meldahl. It was the largest legal payout in Saint Paul history. The agreement would be approved by the City Council in February, 2014 with only a very short public debate. Later that spring, another $20,000 would be agreed to with the family of Lucas Lee for his injuries in the landslide.

A settlement with the St. Louis Park District Schools also soon followed, with the Fofana family receiving $80,000, a matching amount for the Sani family and $40,000 for Meldahl's medical bills. The money from both lawsuits would provide the Fofanas with a beginning for Mohamed's dream projects in Guinea as well as other benefits. For all the families affected by the tragedy, the agreements also brought a certain measure of closure.

But clauses in the two agreements with governmental organizations banned all parties from discussion of the legal case and settlements. That effectively ended public discussion of responsibility and redemption, let alone correction. It was an arrangement that avoided more embarrassment for public officials – particularly in Saint Paul - but also left a cloud of uncertainty in some minds over the entire Lilydale Park incident.

"In a way, I wish we had gone for the full $1.5 million," said Goetz. "(But) we would have had to commit to going to trial for more and the upside was only $500,000 more and there was a definite downside too. … I think we did very well for our clients."

The attorneys received 30 percent commission from the Saint Paul settlement, which left $280,000 apiece for the families of Mohamed Fofana and Haysem Sani, Delvin Meldahl received $140,000 for his injuries. Whether it was sufficient compensation for what happened to the children is open to differing opinions. But the matter was finished as far as the legal system was concerned, with the victims receiving their final compensation.

"They were all very glad to move on," remembered Goetz of his clients. "The Fofanas had a plan for their portion that fit with the kind of people they are."

Several media did pieces on the Fofanas' plan to use much of the settlement awards to honor Mohamed's wishes to see a school built in Guinea. The tone was justifiably favorable and sympathetic to the family's efforts to turn a horrible tragedy into something positive.

But there seemed little interest in whether other positive lessons had been learned after the city paid out over $1 million in taxpayer funds.

On the day of the settlement approval Saint Paul Parks and Recreation spokesperson Brad Meyer would again urge damage control, rather than openness, when asked advice in responding to critics of the city's approach to the Lilydale Park landslide.

"My suggestion would be to not engage," wrote Meyer in an email to Anne Hunt, the Coleman administration's environmental projects coordinator. "If we are forced to respond, I think we keep it to something about the fact that all of this information was included in the report completed by outside investigators immediately following the accident, and as has been the case since the report was released, we continue to stand by the outcome of that very thorough investigation."

He was correct in his short-term focused, cynical advice. Media and most public interest had moved on, again leaving city leaders an unquestioned hand in dealing with Lilydale Park environmental and safety issues. *Pioneer Press* articles would soon turn attention to Saint Paul Parks and Recreation Director Mike Hahm's promises to stabilize the bluff top areas and Brickyard Trail. There would be no follow up on whether and how those goals would be achieved.

Year after year passed. Most of Lilydale Park's bluff areas still remains closed, while the ravine and canyon where the two children died still suffers erosion from

Cherokee culvert storm-water. Physically and emotionally, the scars remain unaddressed. Despite many promises from Mayor Coleman and other officials about developing new "protocols" and safety plans for the future, little has changed except a continued ban on all fossil-hunting.

Just a few weeks after the settlement, in March 2014, a television producer asked for city response to a possible story about city plans to deal with increased numbers of landslides and flood events that might be expected from climate change. It got bounced around in an email chain by Saint Paul's multiple communications personnel. They seemingly didn't know how to answer, or were no longer interested in the subject. The response revealed how quickly opportunities to learn from what had happened in Lilydale Park were being forgotten.

Fire Marshall Steve Zaccard finally answered, honestly. "We're not preparing for that particular hazard, Brandy. Sorry."

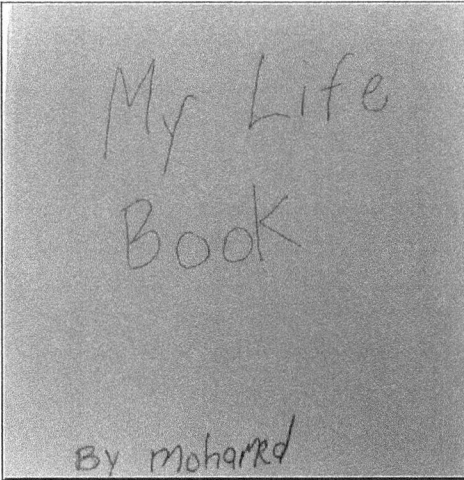

My Life Book

By mohared

Shortly after his death, Mohamed's parents found a booklet full of drawings and stories he had done for a school project. "My Life Book" contained items any 10-year-old American boy might have penned - dreams of sports glory and video games. But it also contained Mohamed's unique vision of how he might help make a better world - including helping the friends he had made in a visit to Guinea, Africa two years before. It was a dream that his family and others are now building upon in his memory.

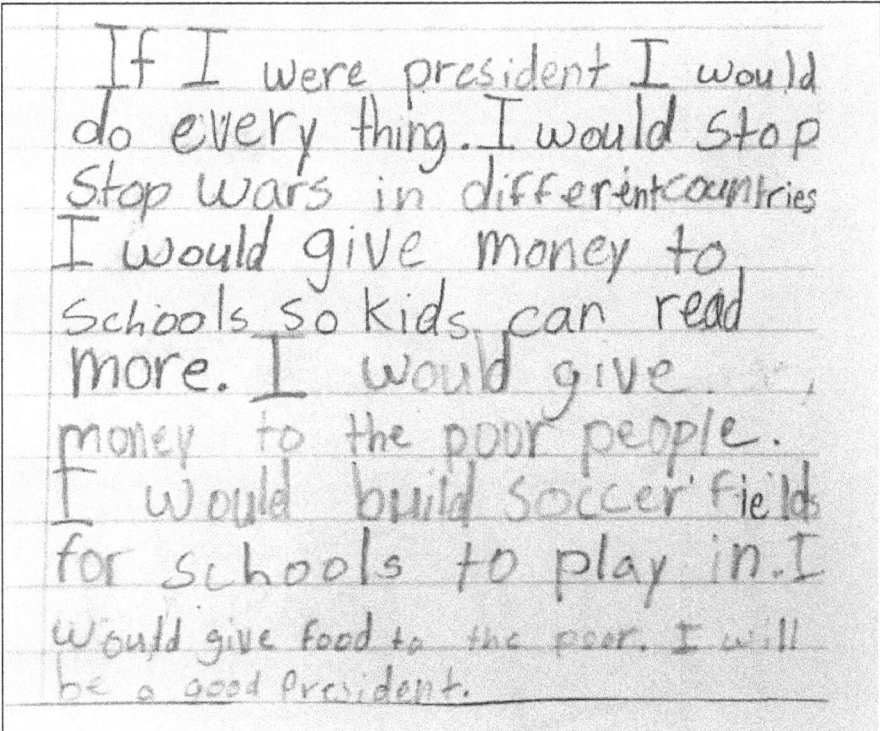

If I were president I would do every thing. I would stop stop wars in different countries I would give money to Schools so kids can read more. I would give money to the poor people. I would build soccer field for schools to play in. I Would give food to the poor. I will be a good President.

My family is fun, interesting. My mom has her own store and is a good cook. My Dad is a a factory worker at supervalue. and tells funny jokes and takes us places.
My aunty owns a store. And she is the boss of the store and she is nice. My uncle is a doctor in St. Louis Park. He helps old people. He helps them When they ave sick or injured.
I Love how interesting my family is.

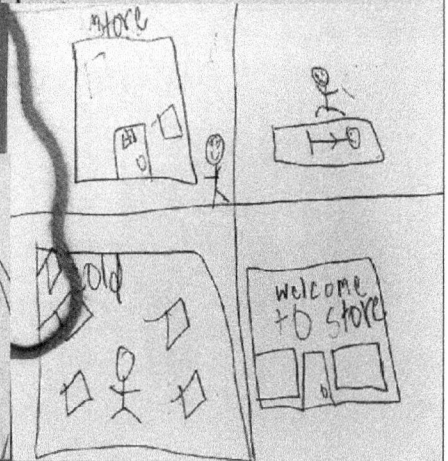

I have lots of hobbies. My first hobby is playing soccer with my brother. My second hobby is playing football with my brothers. My third hobby is reading in my room alone. My fourth hobby is playing video games on my xbox. My last hobby is watching TV. My hobbies are fun and awesome.

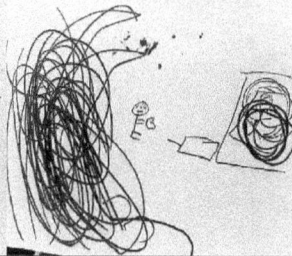

Mohamed's family and friends were alwas first in his short life., as shown in his "My Life Book."

Chapter 9

"I could deny it if I liked. I could deny anything if I liked."
-- **Oscar Wilde,** *The Importance of Being Earnest*

"If we want real forgiveness and healing
we must have real truth."
– **Archbishop Desmond Tutu**

L essons learned from Lilydale. That was the name of a top agenda item for Mayor Chris Coleman's September 19, 2013 staff meeting. It was just two weeks after the release of the Lewis and NTI reports that essentially cleared the City of Saint Paul of any liability for the tragic deaths and injuries to the school children in Lilydale Park.

Such a topic would seem totally appropriate and might be expected to be focused on public safety, parks operation or other future orientation and preventive planning. Perhaps Emergency Management Director Rick Larkin's long-ignored call for an official incident review could have been discussed. We can't absolutely know what was discussed that day since the city did not include any details, minutes or attachments in their response to a Data Practices Act request.

However, a clue may be that the powerpoint presentation was not led by someone like Larkin, but rather by the Mayor's top media spokesperson, Joe

Campbell. It was immediately followed on the agenda by his discussion of "Internal Communications Planning."

Further hints of what the city may now have been most concerned about came in planner Alice Messer's email just four days later, titled "Lilydale Investigation Follow-up Meeting". She wanted top staff of not only Parks and Recreation, but also Public Works leadership, to attend a presentation on Lilydale slope failure investigations. The latter department usually focuses solely on matters such as streets and sewer operation.

Also curiously, the presentation was being led by NTI's Ryan Benson, who had earlier presented the official assessment of the landslide as an entirely natural, unpredictable occurrence. Their conclusion had argued that ground saturation from rainfall had been the main culprit. But subsequent memos from Messer to Saint Paul Parks and Recreation Director Mike Hahm suggested that Benson spent much of his time at the meeting describing human-influenced storm-water as a factor in Lilydale Park bluff instability.

Minnesota DNR geologist Dr. Carrie Jennings briefly joined in these backroom discussions. But her questions about the role of the recently remodeled Cherokee culvert in speeding large amounts of water into the ravine where the landslide occurred, soon made her an unpopular participant. Especially while still facing the likelihood of legal actions, City Hall wasn't about to take a chance on public deviation from the official line put out by the Lewis and NTI reports.

Most PR efforts that fall focused strictly on the city's new roadway and bicycle path improvements in Lilydale

Park with Mayor Chris Coleman sending compliments to Parks and Rec staff. Media coverage by the *Pioneer Press* and others echoed the upbeat tone even while bluff and fossil areas remained closed to the public, as they still are today.

But behind the scenes, concerned staff discussions continued on how to address the bluff's major storm-water problems. They now had a clear sense of urgency.

By January 2014, just about the time a settlement with the Peter Hobart students' families was being reached, the city embarked on its Cherokee Heights Culvert Analysis and Erosion Control Feasibility Study. Messer, in emails, would short-handedly refer to the entire feasibility study as "for the 60-inch culvert at Annapolis and Cherokee Heights Blvd."

Parks and Recreation had been unwilling to pay for a $12,000 study recommended in 2009, but the city now quietly contracted with Barr Engineering for a $93,000 analysis of a portion of the Lilydale Park bluffs. Apparently there were still some legal worries in City Hall. The study had to take the unusual step of first being run through both Saint Paul City Attorney Sara Grewing and Claims Manager Sandra Bodensteiner before going ahead.

Some of the study results, eventually released by Barr in 2015, might explain the nervousness. The engineering firm found that up to 75 percent of all storm-water flowing into Lilydale Park's Brickyard area was coming through the Cherokee Heights culvert. Even more disturbing, their analysis showed peak flow rates that in some cases nearly doubled the estimates of Northern

Technologies Inc. Indeed, the Barr study concluded that high flow rates and velocities were resulting in significant erosion, instability and "causing landslides into the ravine."

Of course, none of this information was ever presented to what would have seemed the most relevant public bodies, including the local West Side Citizens Organization (WSCO) and the Saint Paul City Council. The Saint Paul Parks and Recreation planning staff still controlled most decisions regarding focus of the Cherokee Heights culvert study. Yet the Barr report was officially prepared for, and presented only to, a little-known governmental body called the Lower Mississippi Watershed Management Organization.

Its members included the suburban communities of West St. Paul and Mendota Heights whose storm-water runoff made up most of the flow through the Cherokee Heights culvert. The appointed LMRWMO board was highly influenced by engineering interests and included staff from member cities. Saint Paul's representative during this time was a Public Works employee and few meetings gained any public or media attention.

The body has only very limited, part-time staff of its own, mostly serving as a conduit for state and federal funding of chosen projects. Yet the organization has a theoretical responsibility to help protect the portion of the Mississippi River watershed that includes Lilydale Park.

The LMRWMO would quietly play the lead role in finding funds for Barr's proposal to fortify the ravine below the culvert with rip-rap and concrete. The plan would address the most visible erosion issues near the

Cherokee culvert. But it would do little to decrease the amount of storm-water and sediment running over the bluffs into Lilydale Park and Pickerel Lake.

Curiously, the city would put little pressure on its suburban neighbors to significantly reduce the volume of storm-water running into Saint Paul's jurisdiction. Parks planners would also object, for aesthetic reasons, to highly visible alternatives such as the creation of holding ponds in Cherokee Park to filter sediment and slow water velocity.

Yet another approach, perhaps safest and less environmentally and aesthetically disruptive, called for burying pipes. They would then carry the storm-water down the hillside underground without any erosion of the bluffs.

But that idea was quickly discounted by the city and the LMRWMO as too expensive. Barr would instead be contracted to perform a second stage study looking at potential future multi-million dollar engineering projects. These would include bridges, buttresses, landscaping and other ways to deal with storm-water impacts carrying all the way to the Mississippi River.

Coleman Administration officials were not afraid to think big about their ends, even if they sometimes wanted their means to attract little public attention.

In 2015 Messer, through the LMRWMO, tried to secure $4.6 million in special flood disaster relief funds to apply towards Lilydale Park erosion issues. The highly-competitive federal and state funds were specifically designated only for areas that suffered 2014 flood events. The city proposal was rejected when reviewers realized it was attempting to include the ravine where the two children had died in the 2013 landslide, as well as the nearby 2011 North Knob bluff collapse site.

But the city's creative efforts to find public funding to engineer their way out of problems would continue. So would more erosion damage from engineering decisions, including another highway-related Cherokee bluff drainage project in 2015. Officials again decided to push even more flood-water through the culvert as a solution.

In 2018, the LMRWMO convinced state officials to provide $2.7 million in mostly Legacy funds for projects including the fore-mentioned rip-rap and other "armoring" work in the Lilydale Park ravine. The success of this patch-work approach had already been demonstrated by February 2019, with Barr Engineering reporting back to city staff that part of the "stabilized" channel already was eroding and needed more corrective work.

Even more revealing, they now described how storm-water had created a "scour" hole at the base of the falls very near where Mohamed and Haysem had died. Almost exactly as Dr. Carrie Jennings had witnessed in 2013, soft shale and sandstone was being eroded, resulting in periodic failures of the canyon wall.

Barr even included a photo of a large pile of accumulated rubble and debris as part of their recommendation to seek more funding to pay for more engineering solutions. Again, there was no real discussion of more comprehensive approaches, including reduction of storm-water or underground piping. None of the information would be presented to the Saint Paul City

Council or any truly public body.

Not that it likely would have been seriously challenged. In Lilydale Park it has too often been easier to accept the word of well-paid "experts" rather than confront complex realities involved in protecting an area whose special identity revolves around its mix of human and natural worlds.

Local media had for years been repeatedly reporting promises by Saint Paul Parks and Recreation that Lilydale Park bluffs and fossil areas would be reopening soon. First in 2015 and then again in 2016, the *Pioneer Press* would write front-page pieces that included artistic images of a shored-up river bluff area now made safe for visitors. The 2013 tragedy was always mentioned, but emphasis was on how city staff were now sensitively curbing Mother Nature's unpredictability.

In fairness, Saint Paul did make some improvements to safety in Lilydale Park by 2015. At the urging of former Emergency Management Services Director Rick Larkin, several U.S. National Grid signs were added to the Brickyard Trail area to give hikers a GPS location to use in calling 911. Split-rail fencing was put up along the trail to block usage of unofficial foot paths and "No Hiking" signs were put up in a few restricted areas. Attractive wrought-iron fencing replaced the orange snow fencing that had been left atop Cherokee Park for over a year.

Of course, the simple wire fencing that blocked the entrance to the Vento's View trail was easily torn down by trespassers. When the City of Saint Paul stopped making repairs on the fence, teenagers, dog-walkers and others began unsupervised hiking down the hillside. Homeless persons' campsites could soon be found in not-always-hidden corners, including next to the very canyon where the children had died. All were likely unaware or undeterred by evidence of more rock and mudslides.

A weathered, almost unreadable, sign left from 2013, warning away visitors from the Brickyard Trail, has remained as the only visible connection to the tragedy that still haunts the area. It is almost as if at some point willful amnesia became the official policy of America's Most Liveable City. That marketing mythology is on a Welcome to Saint Paul highway sign near the Cherokee culvert.

It is understandable why some Saint Paul leaders might want to forget about May 22, 2013. But why denial of the event's lessons seems to have included so many, though certainly not all, Saint Paulites, is less clear.

Understandably, many Capitol City residents were confused about conflicting versions of events in a park with which few of them were truly familiar. The psychological shock of hearing about children dying in a public park was also, no doubt, a factor in many otherwise caring citizens wishing the entire incident would go away. In a world where bad news bombards daily, perhaps it was just a natural reaction.

Perhaps it was also a flip side of "Small Paul," a nickname usually used with affection. It refers to the city's charming ability to feel like a collection of small towns with distinct, usually quiet neighborhoods surrounding a relatively small downtown core. The intimacy of relationships in a community where virtually everyone either works in, or knows people who work in local government, was definitely a contributor to many peoples' reluctance to directly challenge public officials. At least one prominent neighborhood activist admitted privately to having been afraid to speak up for fear of losing city contracts in the future.

However, other factors also seemed at play in occasional comments in social media forums and other public places. While most people expressed great sympathy for Peter Hobart students and their parents, more than one Facebook post - including on the Friends of Lilydale Park page – reacted defensively to non-city-residents using a Saint Paul park and then finding fault. Some others suggested a lack of wisdom and common sense on the part of fossil-hunters visiting an area known (by themselves) to be dangerous after periods of rain.

Classic distrust of outsiders or misplaced civic pride? Perhaps. The sentiment was certainly not the norm. Other commenters expressed great empathy for the visitors to Lilydale Park that day and noted that they or their children could easily have been victims of the landslide. Ironically, the West Side neighborhood of Saint Paul would soon help elect a new City Council representative, Rebecca Noecker, who was herself a product of St. Louis Park Schools.

Interest in the tragic deaths of the Peter Hobart Elementary students seemed to fade quickly however. We found that out when our efforts to garner support for some kind of memorial service in the community near the landslide site failed to attract any interest. Again, it was difficult to assess non-reactions. But we couldn't help but wonder if a Saint Paul (or neighborhood) young person had been killed what the local public response might have been.

The fact that both of the victims were non-white and non-Christian are other potential factors deserving consideration. History has provided far too many examples of bias in media and public response to victims who do not belong to dominant social classes.

In fairness, Saint Paul is generally considered one of America's more liberal, racially-harmonious cities. The West Side neighborhood in particular has a long history of accepting people of different backgrounds dating from the 19th Century when it was the place immigrants disembarked at the northern-most port on the Mississippi River. At one time there were reportedly seven major languages spoken in the area and today Spanish and Hmong are common along with English.

But tolerance is clearly under stress in Trump's America. Minnesota Nice has also long been a double-edged characteristic denoting both smiling friendliness and sometimes hidden antagonism. In one perhaps telling on-line exchange, we were told that there wouldn't have been nearly as much official attention given to Mohamed and Haysem's deaths if they hadn't been black. Ironically their skin color didn't merit their being considered Black Lives Matter victims, we were told in another forum. Race is a complicated issue that too often has not been openly addressed.

Whatever the cause, the relative silence of most Saint Paul citizens to news that their city leaders were paying out over $1 million in legal settlements related to the incident was striking. There certainly was concern or anger expressed by some. Others expressed helplessness or a belief that some higher political power would certainly act to address the situation. But too many appeared ready to simply believe the city's official explanations given by paid consultants or generally popular Mayor Chris Coleman.

By contrast, another 2014 legal claim (though not as large as in Lilydale Park) against the city's Saint Paul Parks and Recreation Department drew much more public disgust. That case revolved around the breaking of a lease with a Native American businessman to run a cafe in Como Park. It included allegations that Director Mike Hahm arranged the breakup - along with his then girlfriend, now wife, City Council Member Amy Brendmoen. It was a clear injustice resulting in an $800,000 settlement as well as extended public discussion with calls for heads to roll.

But in the end, there was still no apparent change at in local politics, which has long remained solely in the power of the Democratic Farmer Labor (DFL) Party.

Hahm remained as head of Parks and Brendmoen was re-elected, eventually becoming President of the City Council. City Attorney Sara Grewing would be appointed to a Minnesota judge position by Gov. Mark Dayton, who had previously expressed his great concern for children affected by the Lilydale Park tragedy. Mayor Chris Coleman finished out his third term and felt himself ready to seek Dayton's office. His campaign would soon flounder, but likely not because of any major impact from the handling of the landslide.

I was initially impressed when hearing that Coleman's City Hall staff had, after his election, been told to read

Mary Lethert Wingert's excellent history, "Claiming the City: Politics, Faith, and the Power of Place in St. Paul." The book well conveys how Minnesota's oldest major city incorporated many diverse communities under its wing with a minimum of economic or political divisions, large ghettos, or social conflict. A certain level of tolerance within the city's well-defined neighborhoods helped prevent violent change that racked some other municipalities.

But the flip side of the story was that Saint Paul was often slow to recognize or embrace needed change. Polite citizens sometimes chose to passively follow established leaders even in the face of evidence contradicting their actions or approaches. This soft authoritarianism could, on occasion, be exploited to isolate those who raised questions. In the case of the Lilydale Park tragedy this meant that even many well-educated, self-described progressives would remain neutral, allowing the official City Hall narrative to continue largely unchallenged.

Certainly this was the case in Coleman's 2017 farewell interview with the *Pioneer Press*. Reporter Frederick Melo asked him about the deaths of two children in a city park under his watch. The outgoing Mayor was allowed to pivot the question into a showcasing of his personal family values. There was no further discussion of legal settlements, ongoing Lilydale Park safety issues or even of the disaster's impact on Mohamed, Haysem and their families.

"That hit me as a parent as much as anything. I didn't know if that was my son or his buddies, and that was just really hard," Coleman said, apparently forgetting that 911 reports had from the beginning correctly identified Peter Hobart Elementary students as the victims. He somehow re-imagined the landslide that had come down on St. Louis Park fourth-graders as instead having been a threat to a high-school-aged member of his Saint Paul family.

****

Andrea Lund took a very different lesson from the Lilydale Park tragedy and its aftermath, that truly did directly affect her family. The parent of a fourth grader from Peter Hobart Elementary on the infamous fossil trip, had a very different emotional reaction and opinion of the Coleman administration's legacy.

"Seething rage. ...There was a lot of anger, a lot of anger from those of us who were closest to it. It felt like bullshit," she said, voice shaking, referring to the Lewis and NTI reports commissioned by the Coleman administration. "It felt like here's what we found and here's how we're going to spin it. That's not an investigation, it's a cover-up... It felt insulting. Do you not think people know any better?"

Lund's ire was particularly sparked by what she saw as the City of Saint Paul's focus on avoiding public embarrassment instead of truly prioritizing investigation of what happened to the children.

"They were more concerned about their image than the lives of two little boys," she remembered. "You can't turn back time. But mistakes not learned from and not resolved are doomed to be repeated. This is a lesson of the universe put right in front of peoples' faces and they don't want to do anything about it. That is so Minnesotan it's disgusting."

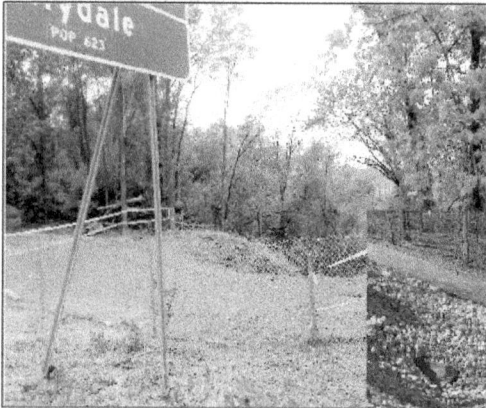

Engineers continue trying to engineer ways to send storm-water over Lilydale Park bluffs. Another Cherokee Park culvert-ravine prject was completed in 2019 at a cost of nearly $1.2 million with trees removed for concrete & rip-rap "armoring" all the way to the Mississippi River. (below.)

Meanwhile engineers note (below left) that the falls near the accident site are now being "scoured" and undercut by the storm-water along with other areas of the ravine that had previously been considered stabilized. More projects are being planned.

To: Doran Hans and Joe Benion
From: John MacDonald
Subject: Lilydale Park channel stabilization erosion.
Date: March 1 2019
Page: 2

Boulevard. A scour hole exists at the base of the falls, where soft shale and sandstone is slowly being eroded, resulting in gradual failure of the face of the falls.

Base of Upper Falls - note rubble and debris

Farther down the channel, a relatively small area of bank erosion is evident in a reach that was previously stabilized by the City. It would be convenient to repair this site in conjunction with the work at the base of the upper falls.

As a result, Lund despaired that the pain would never be fully ended for everyone.

"We probably will never be able to fully bring closure to this incident because there are too many wounds left open," she said. "I think Saint Paul needs to take a hard look at this. But I don't think they want to."

Lund also doubted Coleman's sincerity about victims of the Lilydale Park tragedy "when the cameras weren't there anymore." Even after legal actions were completed, he didn't respond to invitations and other attempts to connect with the Peter Hobart community, she said.

"If this was an indication of his decision-making style then he should have been impeached before he left office," Lund concluded. She described more recent outrage when a Coleman backer at a political event tried to positively describe the ex-mayor's handling of the Lilydale Park tragedy as a reason he should succeed Dayton as Minnesota Governor in 2018.

Another Peter Hobart parent, Derek Riese, described a similar experience at a St. Louis Park DFL precinct caucus with a Coleman campaign aide praising Chris's oversight of investigations into the 2013 deaths of Mohamed and Haysem.

"That took some nerve. I know other people who got physically ill. It just shocked me that anyone would try to promote that as good leadership. I yelled at him," he recounted. "I'm very happy that Chris Coleman is no longer a governor candidate. ...I'm certainly still incensed about the City of Saint Paul."

Interestingly, Jake Spano, Saint Paul's former marketing

director and a self-described believer in Mayor Coleman's "pivot" approach, is now Mayor of St. Louis Park. His attention has long since moved on to other issues such as a controversial Pledge of Allegiance debate.

There are many who now simply want to forget what transpired in Lilydale Park. But Riese believes that many St. Louis Parkers simply remain unclear exactly what to make of the tragedy.

He pointed to media coverage that largely accepted the official line of Saint Paul as the most important factor. Fatigue was another major factor in a community that experienced a total of seven unrelated, but high profile and emotionally-draining, deaths among school district students in the 2012-2014 period.

"My sense was that not that many people were paying attention. I think people were just beaten down," said Riese, noting that official investigations and lawsuits dragged on almost a year. "When I talk to people in St. Louis Park, a lot of them are really surprised when they hear what really happened in Lilydale Park."

Lund agreed, suggesting that many in the Peter Hobart community had been so upset with media that they didn't want to pay attention to coverage beyond the first days. The intense pain and trauma of the event made it hard for many to continue to focus on it.

"Quite honestly, I think a lot of us didn't even want to talk about it after awhile," she admitted.

"People were angry to hear about Saint Paul, but we were too consumed with our immediate pain and concerns," agreed Stacy Atlas, whose daughter had been on the fossil trip.

Anne Schultz, one of the Peter Hobart parents taking the lead in recent years, has seen the problem affecting even their efforts to make something positive from the tragedy.

"That's been the struggle for us. It was obviously a horrible thing. People do not want to talk about it. ...They just want it to go away," she said.

Schultz also primarily blamed Coleman and Saint Paul leaders for lasting impacts resulting from their coverup of key inforation about the events of May 22, 2013.

"It was a terrible accident. But the City of Saint Paul should be held accountable for their negligence. They've passed the buck for too long," she concluded.

But Schultz also faulted media as well as the St. Louis Park School District for letting its understandable concerns about possible legal actions and media criticism stifle reactions. Their timidity in communicating about the Lilydale Park tragedy after the initial days left a public relations void that hurt the entire community.

"I don't think it was the school's fault, they couldn't have known," she said of conditions causing the landslide that struck the fourth grade field trip students. "But there wasn't really any ongoing communication between the District and the rest of Peter Hobart that was affected by the accident. I think it just come down to the District being afraid of a backlash or something legal. ...So we just didn't know what was really going on. Every opportunity for real communication was shut down."

In addition, Schultz believes there was another factor that may have limited interest in serious investigation into the deaths of Mohamed Fofana and Haysem Sani.

"Let's be honest. They are from minority Muslim families. Even though our community is very diverse and says we embrace that, they're two little black boys. Nobody cared about them. You cared if you were from Peter Hobart or if you really knew the story of what happened there. But in general, where's the outrage?" she said. "Had the kids that died, or even the injured, had even one of them been white it would have been a lot different, including the press coverage. ...Here's the headline and now we're done with it."

St. Louis Park, like Saint Paul's West Side neighborhood has long prided itself on being a diverse community. Its history includes a role as the center of the Jewish community in the Scandinavian Upper Midwest. Notable public figures such as the Coen brothers, Thomas Friedman and Al Franken have made lighthearted note of their unique upbringing in a middle-class Minneapolis suburb where it was possible to see people wearing yarmulkas while they ate lutefisk and lefse in a deli.

"St. Louis Park is a weird community," said Reise affectionately. "It feels more like a small town than almost anywhere I've lived. It has a real sense of pride and community and willingness to embrace others. But there's still need and challenges."

Peter Hobart Elementary is itself an International Baccalaureate School, named ironically after another former student who died at a young age in the 1960s. After the landslide there was a brief discussion about renaming the school after Mohamed and Haysem, but a clay sculpture honoring them (in the school's atrium) was decided upon as an alternative.

Today, flags from every nation adorn the hallways of Peter Hobart, along with pictures of children from all ethnic background and slogans in multiple languages. A large banner near the entrance reads in English "International Mindedness – Intercultural Understanding."

The school remains very popular with St. Louis Park parents, including Schultz, who seek for their children an educational experience that prepares them for a diverse world. However, she believes there are lingering effects from the limited community conversations after the 2013 Lilydale Park tragedy.

"Nobody wants to talk about it even now, after the fact. Even when you say we're gonna focus on the good that's coming out of it, nobody really wants to touch that," opined Schultz, pointing to continued problems getting out information about Mohamed Foundation events and activities. She feels it has become harder to keep bonds with Peter Hobart parents and others in the community as the former fourth graders have grown older and moved on to other schools.

In fairness, the District sponsored a major memorial event in 2014 on the May 22 anniversary of the tragedy. Students, teachers, community members and many members of the Saint Paul Fire Department and other first responders held hands and circled Peter Hobart Elementary in commemoration. The District then also unveiled the sculpture in the school's atrium.

By all accounts it was a sweet and bonding moment. But Schultz believes it more necessary than ever that classmates of Mohamed and Haysem be able to continue connecting with each other in order to process accurate information about the landslide event that impacted all of their lives at an early age.

"These kids are connected by that and the School (District) should go out of their way on that anniversary to make sure they are together in one room or place and doing whatever it is they need to do to support them," suggested Schultz. "Those kids are not done with that yet."

Clearly, a number of Peter Hobart parents, teachers and community members are not done processing the event either. The Mohamed Foundation includes a number of people with direct connections to the Lilydale Park tragedy, including Schultz and other parents, including Sandy Boettcher, Stacy Atlas and Melissa Metzler, along with teacher Sarah Reichart. Joining them are other school teachers and community members who certainly were emotionally affected by the event.

However, Schultz is quick to dispel the idea that their bonding is particularly unique. She ties it to another human element of the event and its aftermath.

"I think the unique piece of it, the connecting thread, is the Fofanas. When you get to know them and when you spend fifteen minutes speaking with them, you have no choice," she said with a laugh. "Being part of the St. Louis Park community is a good start but that's not what really gets people motivated and involved. But it's when you hear them that is what makes you want to help them make something better out of all this."

Others totally agree, expressing their admiration and amazement at the positive model created by Mohamed's family of how to respond to tragedy.

"They are some of the most incredible, giving people I've ever met. Every situation while they are still grieving, they were looking out for others," said Atlas, sounding a common sentiment.

"I think a lot of what has happened in the community since then has to do with the Fofanas," agreed Boettcher. "No money is going to bring back your child. But they turned right around and used it for someone else. What American (native born) family is going to do that? There's some but not many. That's what inspires me. This is what the world needs, what the Fofanas did and more people like them."

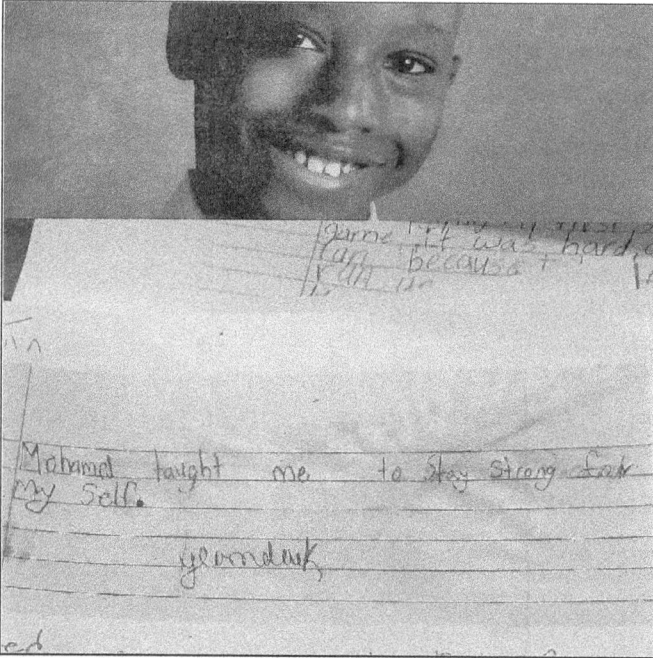

Mohamed was, and is, well remembered by his 4th grade Peter Hobart Elementary classmates, who wrote letters describing his qualities and ways he impacted their lives. Above all, he remains an inspiration to them and many others. It is hoped that the school being built in Mohamed's name in Africa will also act as a cultural bridge between the two different parts of the world.

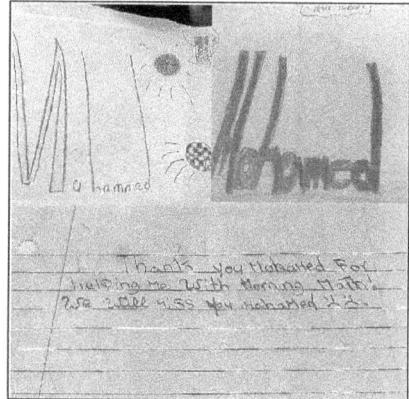

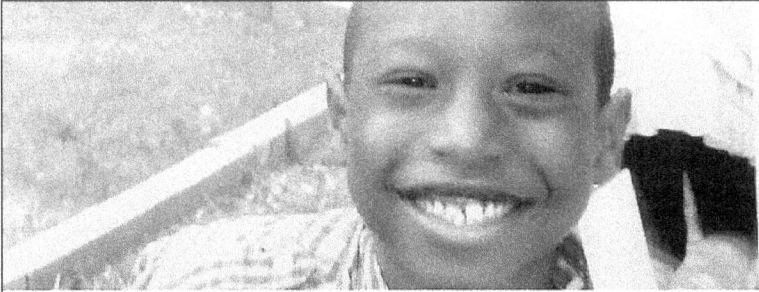

Mohamed was a great Bully Buster and friend. He was soo brave to try to push Derin out of the landslide. He was a great soccer player. I'll never forget him.

His friend,

Nichol

Mohamed was one of my best friend.
Mohamed was a very unique person
Mohamed was very Knowledgable.

From: Sam

Chapter 10

"The truthfulness of the dream is related to the sincerity of the dreamer. Those who have the most truthful dreams are those who are the most truthful in speech."

— **Sahih Muslim Book 017, Hadith Number 4200**

The first days after Mohamed's body was found buried under a landslide in Lilydale Park were undoubtedly more of a dark cloud than a dream. That is the description his parents, Lancine and Madosu, give of the period.

It was a time of grieving and a slow process of trying to comprehend the meaning of his sudden, seemingly senseless death. Friends and family provided valuable consolation. But that alone would never be enough to heal a wound that still remains fresh in many ways.

"You don't feel anything with all the people there. But once they go, every second you feel the pain. ...There is not a day, not an hour goes by that I do not think of that boy," said Lancine of his first son. "I was very angry for the first week and I could not think straight. But we couldn't bring our son back. No. We decided we had to find another way."

That way came from his deep spiritual beliefs and Islamic faith.

"In the Muslim way you have to see God first to ease your pain and be able to handle the situation," he explained. "We believe that if you take it a positive way,

God will make it easier for you."

Madosu agreed, pointing to her faith as the only answer to the intense pain of losing her first born child.

"You have to see Allah (God) first in order to ease your pain and be able to handle situations," she said. "It was very hard but we had to accept and God helps us ease the pain. ...We also have our other kids to take care of. God helped us make it through it all."

Twins Hassan and Al-Seny also felt the pain of Mohamed's loss. Their older brother had been a role model and protector at school, home and everywhere in their young lives. His absence left a void for the eight-year-olds that would not be easily filled.

"They were confused and started fighting at school, which they never did. They are not violent kids. They never even fight with each other," said Lancine of the boys. "They didn't want to talk about Mohamed. But if you don't talk, it's going to be there forever."

The twins were another reason the parents had to focus on the future, rather than the circumstances of Mohamed's death.

"You have to be real, real strong," decided Lancine. "Every day they see my face. If they see my face in pain then they go to school in pain. So I try my best to be strong."

Part of the solution did not come until the following school year. Mohamed's father came up with an idea he hoped would help his surviving sons, one that again demonstrated the Fofana-Kennah family's generosity. Lancine arranged with Peter Hobart Elementary School Principal, Shelley Nielsen, to have Hassan and Al-Seny be part of Sarah Reichart's fourth grade class.

"She was also missing Mohamed so much. ...I thought it would be better for her, seeing the two boys it would also ease her pain," he remembered thinking of connecting Reichart and the twin boys.

The plan succeeded, with benefits going both ways.

"That was a good idea to put them in one class with someone who knew, who understood. They started doing a lot better," remembered Lancine of Hassan and Al-Seny's fourth grade year with Reichart. "She has always been there 24/7 for the twins and us. I can't say enough. ... We are all family."

Mohamed's spiritual presence would continue to be felt in a variety of ways.

His parents described an almost metaphysical presence for the first month or so after the Lilydale Park tragedy. Both describe seeing his figure at night in their home, and having other sensations that indicated their deceased son was still somehow with them.

"The first 30 days or so after Mohamed passed, sometimes when I get in my room I smelled like a perfume smell," said Lancine, with Madosu nodding in agreement.

"We could hear sounds in the bedroom and I could just feel his presence," his mother added, noting that other family members had reported similar feelings or had even seen Mohamed in the days immediately after his death. Lancine is also quick to describe how at a school birthday party nearly a year later, one of his deceased son's classmates suddenly stopped and pointed across the room to where he believed he saw Mohamed.

Such after-life phenomena have been reported in many cultures and places, as anyone who watches cable TV can confirm. Ghosts appear in the Bible and nearly one in five Americans now believes in ghosts or spirits, confirming that the concept crosses faiths and oceans. But accounts of Mohamed's apparition might also be interpreted as fitting with some African animist cultural beliefs, or perhaps the Islamic concept of the Qareen, a spiritual double every human has that exists in a parallel dimension.

Regardless, the Fofanas obviously remained very close to Peter Hobart Elementary and vice versa – certainly keeping Mohamed's presence alive in that sense. However, it wasn't until Madosu was looking through some of his class papers and personal items, sent home after the Lilydale Park tragedy, that the strongest link to the future was discovered.

"I was so surprised. I said 'Lancine, come here and look at this,'" she remembered of a small, hand-made journal neither of the parents had ever before seen. "It was very emotional. But I was happy to learn what he wanted to do with his life."

"My Life Book" was the title Mohamed had printed on the front in large letters. Inside was a combination of drawings and handwritten, short thoughts the 10-year-old had composed. Subjects included his family, his love for sports and games, and his goals for the future. Some of those goals were typical of a young boy – such as growing up to be a famous professional soccer player. Other subjects included his love for his mother's cooking. Still different thoughts showed a concern for others and a wisdom well beyond his years.

In particular, Mohamed made a large point of

describing how he envisioned someday being in position to make life better for the world, and especially for impoverished children in places like Guinea and Liberia.

"If I were president I would do everything. I would stop wars in different countries. I would give money to schools, so kids can read more. And I would give money to the poor people. I would build soccer fields in schools where kids can play. I would give food to the poor. I will be a good president," he wrote in his journal, expressing youthful self-confidence about his future life.

It was a dream that clearly sprang from, and was consistent with, Mohamed's actions during his several-week visit to Siguiri, Guinea less than two years before his death. The eight-year-old had traveled there with his mother to meet African family members for the first time.

It was his first encounter with widespread poverty, shortages of food, lack of educational opportunities and other human problems in a developing country. It would have been an intimidating and possibly even repulsive experience for an average American-born young person. But Mohamed, with his altruistic outlook, was clearly not an average young man.

"Everywhere we went, he just wanted to give away his food, his clothes, money," recalled Madosu with a laugh. "'Mother, why they don't have any shoes, why they don't go to school,' he'd say. Mohamed kept coming to me asking for more money. "

Despite not speaking any of the Mandingo language when he arrived in Guinea, he was soon out playing soccer with many new friends. Mohamed is still remembered in Siguiri for his humility and down-to-earth attitude, despite his obvious material advantages when he returned to the U.S.

"He was just like me. We played football (soccer) together. We ran on the street together. He was fun, always happy and nice," said Mamadou Camara, a Guinean relative who had been about Mohamed's age in 2009. "I will always remember him."

That sentiment is widespread on both sides of the Atlantic Ocean.

Mohamed's journal became a special inspiration for making sure others would long remember him. His spirit of caring for others, and his desire to help children without a school, soccer fields and other opportunities in life became the beginning of a movement. The messages from his journal made clear a way to make something positive result from his passing.

"I said to Madosu, we have to do this. We have a chance to make his dream come true," recalled Lancine, referring to proceeds from 2014 legal settlements with the City of Saint Paul and St. Louis Park School District. Mohamed's tragic death would give life to plans for a school and programs in Guinea that would carry forward his name and legacy.

The project was announced and initial efforts got underway with enthusiasm.

Through family members in Siguiri, Lancine was able to secure a sizable piece of land on the edge of the mining boom town. Children in the poor, nearby village had almost no realistic school options. They could walk nearly five miles in the hot sun along a dangerous road every day, or they could move into the city away from their families. Even then, most Guinea public schools are severely underfunded and have few supplies, few desks and sometimes not even any teachers on days when government payroll cutbacks have forced them to work second jobs.

The Fofanas decided they couldn't think small. They wanted a full-service school for up to 300 students in kindergarten though sixth grade. Eventually they might expand to grades seven through 12. Subjects will include history, math, and science with French and English in higher grades. Most importantly, the school will have a sliding fee scale for students and families. This will hopefully allow even the most impoverished children to receive not only education, but other basic needs such as meals and health care at a school clinic. After-school programs will serve parents and the community.

"It will be a private school for those who can pay, but half of those students we will rescue from the streets," proudly promised Lancine, noting it was to be part of Mohamed's plan. "This will be a very good school, with good teachers and not too many students in each classroom so they can really learn. ...And, of course there will be soccer and sports."

Using only funds from the legal settlements, the Fofanas started construction on the physical shell of the structure. Cement block walls and initial building infrastructure went up relatively quickly. Family and immediate friends at home in Minnesota, such as Kurt Swanson and Andrea Cloud, helped them begin working on the ambitious plan.

Groundbreaking and construction work on the school began several years ago but has been stalled for lack of funds. Mohamed Fofana Memorial Foundation board members remain determined that the effort will continue however. Most recently a community clinic, which will also serve the school, has neared opening with receipt of donated medical equipment and supplies.

MOHAMED
FOFANA
MEMORIAL SCHOOL

CONNECTING COMMUNITIES
ACROSS THE WORLD

VIEW OF FRONT ENTRANCE

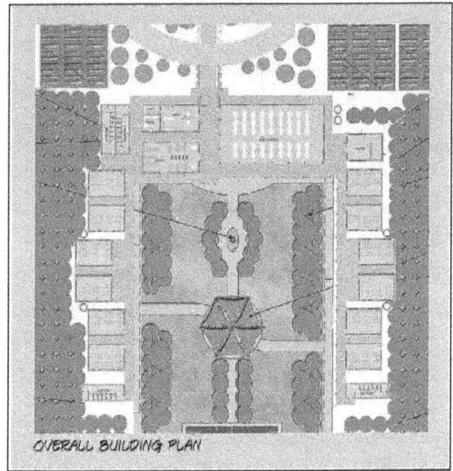
OVERALL BUILDING PLAN

AXONOMETRIC VIEW

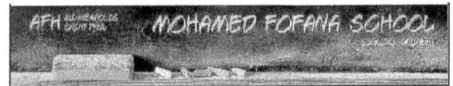
MOHAMED FOFANA SCHOOL

Mohamed Fofana Memorial Foundation school plans include a library, media center, indoor and outdoor basketball court, a landscaped courtyard with amphitheater, and a full sized soccer field. It will serve 300 students from kindergarten through sixth grade. The campus facilities will have a large, multi-purpose room multiple classrooms, adult education classes and more rooms allowing it to become a true community center after school hours.

But as visions and costs grew, they knew that they would need more help. They didn't need to look far for their first allies. Peter Hobart teachers and parents, beginning with Sarah Reichart, quickly jumped into the void and helped spread the word. The winning sales pitch came from the Fofana-Kennahs with their infectious optimism.

Indeed, at times Lancine can sound like an African-born, Islamic Norman Vincent Peale preaching the power of positive thinking. Mohamed's death had not been an ending but would be the start to something greater, his father described confidently.

"From the beginning I knew that if we kept thinking positive, God would bring good," Lancine said. "Now he has brought us all these good people."

Of course, success also requires good people being willing to work.

"I was just thrilled when Sarah and the St. Louis Park teachers came on board," said Swanson, whose mission experience in Africa has made him a key connection between the two different cultures. "It's gonna be an incremental process."

Together the group formed a non-profit foundation in 2015 with the help of local attorneys providing pro bono assistance. Soon they were connected with another professional organization contributing its time. Architecture For Humanity contributed its expertise in developing designs for the school and all its facilities.

"It's just a great group that has come together trying to make something positive out of this tragedy," concluded Derek Burrows Reise, who also assisted with getting the

Foundation's non-profit status. "They're all determined to get it done and continue on."

Plans now call for a library, media center, indoor and outdoor basketball court, a landscaped courtyard with amphitheater, and a full sized soccer field. The campus facilities will have a large, multi-purpose room multiple classrooms, adult education classes and more rooms allowing it to become a true community center after school hours. Medical equipment for the clinic has also been collected and sent to Guinea.

The design process has required long meetings for everyone interested in making the Mohamed Fofana Memorial School a reality. It was also a bonding process that brought together a mix of people and ideas.

That would only be the beginning. A logo, calendar, t-shirts, a website (*http://mohamedsdream.com*), Facebook page and other publicity materials were designed and distributed. Legal filings and other organizational requirements meant many hours of attention from the group of volunteers, busy with their own career and family obligations.

But memories of Mohamed clearly inspired those joining the virtual Fofana family. A video captured students' and teachers' thoughts about the uniqueness of a 10-year-old who was well-remembered after his untimely death. Classmates described his sense of humor, his competitiveness in soccer balanced against his good sportsmanship and his willingness to share anything from snacks to helping with homework. His spirit of giving back was also clearly living on through those who would not soon forget him.

"Mohamed was not like any other ordinary friend," said former Peter Hobart fourth-grader Eric Perez. "He was something more. He was like family."

Others in the video described him as an ongoing inspiration.

"Mohamed loved to learn. He wanted everybody to have that same opportunity," said Shannon Alexander, a Peter Hobart parent and a chaperone on the Lilydale Park trip. "So for him to have that wish would be fulfilling for anybody who was any part of it."

The foundation bearing Mohamed's name began to raise funds. They set an ambitious target of at least $400,000 to meet capital needs and a multitude of other costs, including hiring of qualified Guinean teachers and other staff, the purchase of desks, computers, teaching materials and other ongoing operational needs. Strong administration of school and community programs will be another requirement, of course with the Fofana family in Guinea also always there in support.

As with any project, costs and other issues have continued to arise since groundbreaking got underway. Availability of materials in Guinea and approaches to construction that differ from those in the U.S. can readily require changes to plans originating in North America. Maintaining high standards and long-term fundraising approaches, even when it means delays in building, can be hard to understand for those in a developing country. Sometimes rushing ahead, even if it brings inferior results, seems the sensible approach to those without a history of assurance that there will be more resources coming.

"The challenge has sometimes been to match up the

two cultures," admitted Swanson, whose past mission work experience and residence in Guinea has been invaluable. "I'm still confident, but we've got a lot of things to do."

The contrast in perspectives was evident during my own brief visit to Siguiri. Villagers at the project site enthusiastically rushed to meet visitors they were hopeful would bring news the school is soon to open, even if only partially built.

But they patiently nodded their understanding, as Lancine described how the North American group continues to raise funds so construction of the building can resume and move toward completion. Any disappointment was quickly replaced with warm hospitality. Smiles were in abundance later that day when the visitors are hosted at a soccer game and ceremonies, with seemingly the entire nearby community of several hundred people attending and sharing humble refreshments.

On a following day, we stopped at a Siguiri vocational school of sorts, where several dozen young women sit around about a dozen sewing machines in a non-air-conditioned room. Two volunteer instructors explained that the students are all impoverished former prostitutes or other street dwellers, struggling to learn an alternative skills. But there are often no supplies for the rented machines and the young women had not had any breakfast or lunch.

We gave a donation that was insufficient, but possibly allowed them all to eat for several days. Lancine gave a brief talk about keeping hope in the value of education. It clearly left several pairs of teary eyes, including mine.

"We've got to figure out how to do this," said Lancine determinedly. "The (Guinea) government really doesn't care. We have to do it."

That spirit has touched many on both sides of the Atlantic.

The Minnesota-based foundation board members have had successes as well as setbacks in their fundraising efforts. Generous initial community support can sometimes be hard to sustain in a fast-moving world of many pressing needs and distractions.

Initial publicity in local media gave an early boost, along with online efforts. Ice cream socials, house parties and other grassroots efforts have been amazingly successful on many occasions. Mohamed's compelling story pulls at hearts and purse strings.

But monthly meetings need continue at Peter Hobart Elementary with board members sharing ideas and network contacts in a search for well-heeled donors – or at least those with connections to wealth.

Naturally, there are frustrations. Bad weather, slow or non-responses from celebrity figures or potential benefactors and general bad luck are a normal part of any nonprofit's life. Foundation members remain generally upbeat, perhaps taking their cues from the irrepressibly positive spirit of the Fofanas. Lancine and Madosu, along with 12-year-old Hassan and Al-Seny, often attend. But moments of discouragement can slip through when they realize the size of their undertaking.

"It's a huge project. All the time it's daunting. If it wasn't, I'd be delusional," said Anne Schultz, chair of the foundation. "You just have to keep plugging along one baby step at a time. When you run out of steam someone else picks it up for awhile."

But a ticking clock may be another factor for the Mohamed Fofana Memorial Foundation. Original dates for opening the school have come and gone, potentially threatening momentum. With the passing of years and memories of the Lilydale Park tragedy, as well as the other seemingly endless social and political distractions of American life, a deceased young boy's vision can start to seem less important.

"Time and tragedy is a bit of a challenge," noted Sara Thompson, Communications Director for the St. Louis Park School District, noting that Peter Hobart students from Mohamed's class have now all graduated from elementary school. "Some people want to move on and others feel we have to remember."

But she assured that "The District certainly doesn't see it as something that needs to be left behind. It's an important part of our history."

Foundation leaders and the Fofana family see Mohamed's vision not just as history but as an ongoing connection to the future. They point to potential connections with the Guinea school as furthering Peter Hobart's ongoing role as an International Baccalaureate school. Students sharing pen-pal connections, art projects, even joint classes via the internet are seen as the first step. Eventually there might be student trips to West Africa, teacher exchanges between the two schools, and other learning partnerships.

"St. Louis Park has always been an accepting place. But now we have another opportunity to accept and learn from other people. ...This is what I want us to be, a place where we share what we are doing and whatever they are doing," said board member Stacy Atlas. "It is our chance. Mohamed gave us this chance."

Mohamed's legacy could go even further than what the 10-year-old described in his journal.

"I see the potential of this project to be more than just a school," agreed board chair Schultz. "It will become this amazing symbiotic example of two cultures connecting and learning from each other. ...We will have created an amazing model and legacy."

Not that building only to Mohamed's original vision would be a failure.

"If it just becomes a normal school that would be great," concluded Swanson, referring to the extreme shortage of any educational opportunities in Guinea. "But we have a chance to do a lot more."

Getting there is, of course, the challenge.

"There are times when it seems like we're never going to do this because it's just so hard. But we want this so bad, we're not giving up," said board treasurer Sandy Boettcher. "You just have to stay at it and maybe you'll meet that person, just the right one. Or maybe someone else will help pick up the cause and carry it on."

Timelines are made to be broken in an effort like this. But board members acknowledge they'd like to keep moving to a conclusion in the near future.

"I'd really like to have this (Guinea school building) by the time our kids graduate from high school before they get older and move on," admitted Boettcher, referring to the former fourth grade classmates of Mohamed. "But who knows, maybe they'll be the ones to take it on."

Indeed, the next generation is already picking up the baton in the form of Mohamed's younger brothers Hassan and Al-Semi. The twins have not only been active board members but have conducted their own fundraising drives among fellow students. They talk of some day becoming teachers or administrators at the Guinea school.

"I will be principal," said Hassan, teasing his twin brother.

"OK, then I will be soccer coach," responded Al-Seny.

But the seriousness of fulfilling Mohamed's vision has clearly been passed down from his parents. Their deceased eldest son lives on as a role model for the twins in words and deeds.

"Even sometimes when we have a family meetings we talk about Mohamed as an example. ...Whenever he did something wrong we told him, and he never did it twice," remembered Lancine, with Madosu nodding in affirmation. "He will always be with us."

If that lesson hasn't yet been learned by everyone involved in the Lilydale Park tragedy, Mohamed's example lives on in others' efforts to work for something bigger than themselves. Learning from the past in order to make a better future was always what mattered, insist the Fofanas.

"The money is nothing. Nobody can pay for Mohamed. We wanted to make his dream come true," recalled Madosu of the lawsuit outcome. The landslide would not bury his dream of making the world a better place.

"So something good can come out of a sad thing," added Lancine. " This was a tragedy. But out of that can come a school for other kids who really need it. How many people can do that?"

Mohamed's dream will be achieved against all odds, the Fofana family and other backers unanimously insist. Their determination makes it easy to believe. But in many ways, his legacy may have already been established even if the Guinea school is never completed.

"We are inter-connected. We all affect each other and share this global world," summarized Atlas. "This is what Mohamed taught us. This is the lesson we're learning. It is the gift Mohamed gave us."

In the end, a ten-year-old's vision was a dream that can come true for everyone willing to be part of it.

"Mohamed was not just for us. He was for the school and everybody," agreed his father. "We are all the same family."

Mohamed Fofana Memorial Foundation board members and supporters continue their grassroots campaign for the school and medical center through a variety of house parties, ice cream socials and other fundraising efforts. Below right, Lancine Fofana celebrates the contribution of life-saving medical equipment that has already been transported to Guinea, West Africa.

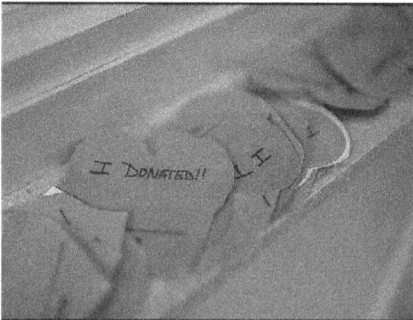

http://mohamedsdream.com

About the Author

Jon Kerr is a long-time journalist and writer who also happened to be a community, historical and environmental advocate for Lilydale Park where the landslide occurred. He has become close with Mohamed's family and is now part of the Dream, along with others engaged in an effort crossing cultures and oceans.

His previous pieces on the Lilydale landslide were published in *City Pages* (Minneapolis). *He has* two published books that can be foundon Amazon: *Calvin: Baseball's Last Dinosaur* (1990) and *Mark Twain and the River of Timeless Temptation* (2017).

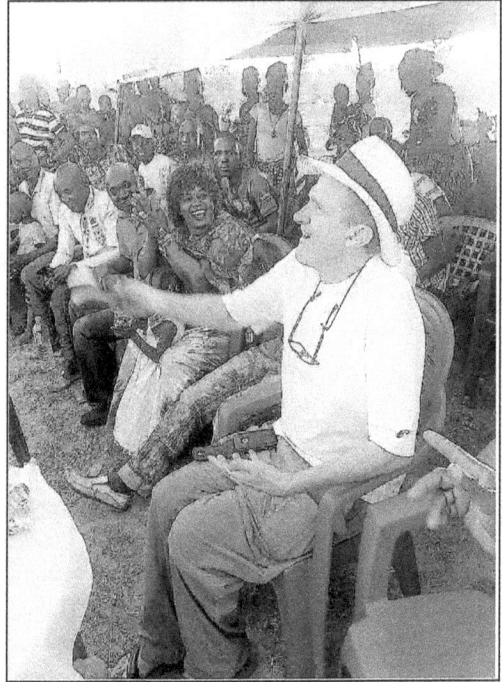

www.ingramcontent.com/pod-product-compliance
Lightning Source LLC
Chambersburg PA
CBHW021140090426
42740CB00008B/870